Devotional Companion

to the
International Lessons
2002–2003

Usable with all Popular Lesson Annuals

Jeffrey A. Rasche

ABINGDON PRESS / Nashville

DEVOTIONAL COMPANION TO THE INTERNATIONAL LESSONS 2002–2003

Copyright © 2002 by Abingdon Press

This book is printed on acid-free paper.

ISBN 0-687-09949-8
ISSN 1074-9918

02 03 04 05 06 07 08 09 10 11 — 10 9 8 7 6 5 4 3 2 1

MANUFACTURED IN THE UNITED STATES OF AMERICA

Hymnals Referenced

B   Forbis, Wesley, ed. *The Baptist Hymnal*. Nashville: Convention Press, 1991.

C   *The Cokesbury Worship Hymnal*. Nashville: Abingdon Press, 1966.

E   Glover, Raymond, ed. *The Hymnal 1982*. New York: The Church Hymnal Corporation, 1985.

F   Bock, Fred, ed. *Hymns for the Family of God*. Nashville: Paragon Associates, Inc., 1976.

L   *Lutheran Book of Worship*. Minneapolis: Augsburg Publishing House, 1978.

P   McKim, LindaJo, ed. *The Presbyterian Hymnal*. Louisville: Westminster/John Knox Press, 1990.

UM   Young, Carlton R., ed. *The United Methodist Hymnal*. Nashville: The United Methodist Publishing House, 1989.

W   Batastini, Robert J., ed. *Worship*. Chicago: GIA Publications, 1986.

READ IN YOUR BIBLE: *Psalm 122:1-9*   **September 1, 2002**
SUGGESTED PSALM: *Psalm 63:1-5*
SUGGESTED HYMNS:
  "Blest Be the Tie That Binds" *(B, C, F, L, P, UM)*
  "Let Us Break Bread Together" *(B, E, F, L, P, UM, W)*

A Time to Decide

Hearing the Word

Have you ever traveled a distance to attend a major league ball-game, or perhaps stepped into a large arena after a long trip to be part of a massive concert or rally? This psalm captures the excitement of such an event. The Temple was an architectural marvel. Most people from the outlying small towns would not have seen anything like it without traveling to Jerusalem; it would be a little like a youth who comes from a town without a stoplight or a building more than two stories tall visiting New York City! Of course, the joy of being in that physical place was secondary to simply knowing that the Temple was the Lord's house, and the spiritual center of their faith. Psalm 122 goes perfectly with the scripture for today's lesson (from 2 Chronicles), in which King Hezekiah summons all the Israelites to come to Jerusalem to renew their faith.

Living the Word

Psalm 122 expresses the excitement of a layperson about coming to worship. Therefore, I suspect a preacher wrote the psalm! After all, we who are preachers certainly hope that our church members feel excited about coming to worship! But if they all do feel excited about coming to church, then where do all the jokes come from about falling asleep in church and keeping the sermon shorter? Is there any grain of truth in that line of humor?

Once during a pastoral prayer I gave at church, I must have been boring a little child. Several times during my prayer, he cried out (plenty loud for the whole congregation to hear), "Amen." This was followed by failed attempts to cover up chuckling by adults who knew they were supposed to be serious and quiet. The more I tried to keep my composure and carry on (knowing I was supposed to be serious and quiet too), the more the little boy kept interrupting the prayer with an insistent "Amen." Even the mother's hand clamped over his mouth could not hide the truth—he was bored, and let everybody know it!

The psalmist wrote, however, "I was glad when they said to me, 'Let us go to the Lord's house' " (122:1). So what made him feel glad and excited? Did he just have a more entertaining preacher, better musicians, maybe a big screen video in his church?

No, unless you assume that the church is just another form of entertainment, then these things miss the point. The church is not in the entertainment business, but that may be a prevailing notion in today's technological culture. Look at churches as they appear on television. They have close-up shots, spotlights, sound effects, video clips of hungry children, professional-caliber singers, and backup musicians. They even have commercial breaks!

But worship is not meant to entertain us; it is meant to bring us closer to God. It is really not up to the preacher as much as it is up to us. Even if we can't get any new insight from the sermon, we can still draw near to God in the singing and the silent prayer. If we give God the chance, God will change us, challenge us, teach us the meaning of real love, help us carry our burdens, give us the gift of a supportive community of faith, fill us with a strong sense of mission, renew our strength, and fill us with the new life of Jesus Christ. For that, we do not need to be entertained; we just need to open our heart to God.

You may not feel like shouting "Amen" in every prayer. Maybe your church has a live marching band and a tag team of shouting acrobatic preachers. But if not, it is still good to go to the Lord's house. For even without the commercial breaks and lush potted plants and spotlights, God has come to be with you, too. And it is God's presence with us, not the entertainment value, that makes it so good for us to go to the Lord's house and worship.

Let us pray:
Lord, when worship is interesting and emotionally powerful, we thank you for the excitement of mountaintop experiences. But we also thank you for being there to work with us and surround us with your loving, life-changing presence even when worship seems routine and ordinary. May we be found by you, every time we turn to you in worship. Amen.

READ IN YOUR BIBLE: *2 Chronicles 6:36-42*   **September 8, 2002**
SUGGESTED PSALM: *Psalm 123*
SUGGESTED HYMNS:
   "Just As I Am, Without One Plea" (B, C, E, F, L, P, UM)
   "Amazing Grace" (All)

Learning the Hard Way

Hearing the Word

When King Solomon dedicated the Temple, he offered a long prayer (2 Chronicles 6:14-42). King Solomon imagines various reasons why people might need the Temple in the future, and asks God to listen to the prayers of the people in those situations. Today's devotional scripture features a part of that prayer where Solomon speaks of someone who has been "evicted" by God from the promised land; in that case he asks God to hear that person's prayer of repentance even from far away and restore them to the promised land. It is no accident, then, that today's lesson scripture that is a few chapters later in 2 Chronicles (33:1-13) is about the time when King Manasseh went through that same cycle of sin, punishment through eviction, repentance, and restoration to the promised land.

Living the Word

In the middle of the afternoon a frustrated landlord tapes a sign to an apartment door. "Eviction Notice." When the tenant comes home from work, he sees the sign, the angry red letters, the deadline to move out of there, the cold legal threats. What happened to the good relationship with the apartment owner, the warm welcome letter, the kindly father figure who stayed late one day to help him paint the kitchen and living room walls?

In a word, the relationship went sour because of the tenant's broken promise. Instead of mailing the rent in full and on time, he delivered partial payments only after considerable nagging, and lots of excuses. At first the landlord understood, but eventually his patience wore out and the relationship, which could have been good, turned bad. It ended in eviction; kicking the tenant out of the "promised land" for not living up to his promises. So, is it too

7

late at this point for the relationship between tenant and landlord?

That is essentially what happened to Manasseh. He was evicted from the promised land for not living up to his promises. Then, in exile and a prisoner of the Assyrians, he realized how badly he had messed up his life, and how badly he had let God down. The question: "Was it too late for him?" How might this situation apply to people we know, or might encounter, in twenty-first century America? Who are the "evicted" of American society? Who might feel that they have "blown it," and have no hope of restoring a broken relationship?

I think first of criminals. They are caught, convicted, and literally "evicted" from society by being thrown in prison. It is not popular these days to have any sympathy for them at all. They can pray for forgiveness in prison, but that does not guarantee they will get out any sooner. So, in your Bible, what does Jesus say about visiting the sick and imprisoned? One of the least common ministries in many churches is outreach to those in prison; so, do we just leave them in exile?

Then there are those sins that don't make the gossip column in the town coffee shop. In fact, sins nobody knows about except God. We know we have messed up in a way that we can never go back and change. We must live with the pain of kicking ourselves around the block mentally, or suspecting that if people knew the real truth about who we are without our "Sunday morning shine," they might not accept us any longer. So our sin silently drags us out of the promised land into a private, tortured exile. Can God forgive even the sins for which we cannot forgive ourselves?

I guess that's the question. Is there such a thing as a sin so terrible that even God cannot forgive it? Even if society sees eviction as the only option, can God find a way to restore us to the promised land? And if God can do that for us, what would it mean if we truly believed God could do that for others, too? We know about eviction. But is there hope after the eviction notice is up? There was hope even for Manasseh; has God changed so much since then?

Let us pray:
Lord, help us truly believe that you never run out of hope for us. Help us act toward others as though every person is redeemable. Help us receive, and believe in, the awesome power of your forgiving, renewing, life-giving love. Amen.

READ IN YOUR BIBLE: *Isaiah 55:6-11*   **September 15, 2002**
SUGGESTED PSALM: *Psalm 50*
SUGGESTED HYMNS:
 "Holy, Holy, Holy" (All)
 "Thine Be the Glory" (B, F, L, P, UM)

Overcoming Spiritual Complacency

Hearing the Word

Today's devotional and lesson scriptures come from opposite ends of the same event. That event is the Babylonian Exile in approximately 586 B.C. In it the Babylonians crushed Judah, including the Temple and the holy city of Jerusalem. They took the Israelites who survived as captives and forced them to resettle outside of their promised land. The lesson scripture (from Zephaniah chapters 1 and 3) is the prophet's warning to the Israelites about the coming judgment. Even though the Northern Kingdom of Israel had already fallen years before to the Assyrians, the Israelites living in Judah were complacent and felt safe because they had the Temple in their midst. After the disaster came, Isaiah addressed the exiles in chapters 40–55, which includes today's devotional scripture. He assured them there was still hope, but they needed to turn to God "while God was near."

Living the Word

One of the great challenges for many Americans today is losing weight. French fries and ice cream just taste too good, and they are too plentiful. On top of that, we sit a lot.

Of course, the real enemy is not French fries and sitting—it is complacency. We know what we need to do to lose weight, and why it is good for us. For those who are couch potatoes, countless television shows feature medical "prophets" preaching about the difference between "good fats" and "bad fats," the benefits of daily aerobic exercise, and the dangers of ignoring these warnings.

Complacency means that we understand what the prophets are saying, and we might even agree with their message. But we simply figure that one more little French fry won't make that much difference. Tomorrow seems like a better day to start that diet.

Likewise, we often have religious beliefs or plans to grow spiritually that seem easy to put off until tomorrow. They just aren't urgent enough to deal with "today." What this really means is rejection of God's will. Instead of an outright rejection, though, it is rejection by combining agreement with procrastination. If you believe that that devil is an active force in the world, then surely this would have to be one of the most effective weapons in his arsenal. Let good people have their good intentions. Let them have their beliefs, and agree with God's ideas wholeheartedly. Just let them be complacent enough to make God's ideas wait until tomorrow.

How would you keep millions of Christians from feeding the masses of starving people in Third World countries? Complacency will do just fine. How would you let a visitor to the church question whether or not they were truly accepted, and finally give up on the church? Complacency will help all the members think, "Oh, surely they know they are welcome without me going over there to talk to them."

The prophets, of course, take the other side. They insist that the time is now—not tomorrow—to do God's will. They say it really matters what you do, and that we need to open our eyes to see how God wants us to change our lives. You know, those old prophets probably were not much fun to be around; they always made sure you knew they were speaking on God's behalf. They would probably fuss at you for eating even one more French fry, or waiting even one more day to feed the starving, or letting even one chance to greet a visitor go by, or living by the philosophy down at church, "if it ain't broke, don't fix it."

An added thought from "the friendly opposition": Hey! The writer sure has expressed some powerful ideas here, don't you think! Perhaps you will agree with them, and think about putting them into action—say, sometime this coming week—or maybe the next?

Let us pray:
Lord, when it comes to doing your will, help us feel the urgency of doing it now. Amen.

SUGGESTED PSALM: *Psalm 119:9-16*

SUGGESTED HYMNS:

"*Have Thine Own Way, Lord*" *(B, C, F, UM)*

"*Lift Every Voice and Sing*" *(B, E, L, P, UM, W)*

What You Don't Know Can Hurt You

Hearing the Word

Psalm 119:1-8 could very well express the feelings that King Josiah had in the story we find in today's lesson scripture (2 Chronicles 34–35). It is amazing to us to imagine a child only eight years old becoming king, as was the case with Josiah. It is even more amazing that he had the desire to "clean house" and get rid of the idols he had inherited from his parents. Just imagine him gathering all the people of Israel, a child king, and making them swear that from now on they would be obedient to God alone, and stop worshiping the idols. Psalm 119 expresses a deep love for God's ways, and the hope of a young person that as they live out their life they will be able to keep God's laws faithfully.

Living the Word

I recently heard a professor give a lecture where he marveled about how a huge airplane can rush down the runway and fly into the air like a bird. After all, how much does a 767 weigh? Then, as this huge machine sits on the ground, it receives truckload after truckload of cargo including fuel, food, supplies, and one bulging bag of luggage after another. Finally, two hundred or more people march on board, and this gargantuan machine, stuffed to the brim, is supposed to leap off the ground and into the sky!

He pointed out that this feat depends on the interaction of two basic forces. The first is gravity. Unless you leave the earth's atmosphere and travel a long distance away through space, the power of gravity is always at work. It exerts its pull on any and

11

every object, from satellites circling the earth to an Olympic diver doing flips before plunging into the water.

The second force at work on the plane is lift. The curve of the wing disturbs the flow of air over the top of the wing, creating a pocket of lower air pressure. This makes the air below the wing, which is at a higher air pressure, push upward toward the lower air pressure, lifting the plane. This same principle can be seen in the effect of air on a shower curtain. When the shower is off, the air pressure is the same on both sides of the curtain, and it hangs straight. But when the shower is turned on, the rush of water makes air turbulence, which lowers the air pressure inside the shower. Therefore, the air outside the shower curtain pushes in.

All along the airplane journey, these two forces are still at work. Gravity doesn't disappear just because lift is stronger at the moment. In fact, if lift ever decreases, gravity will be able to exert its power on the path of the aircraft. In our life, there are also opposing forces at work. Psalm 119 speaks of the importance of following the law of the Lord. You might say that following God's law tends to add lift to our life, not just in the sense of making us heaven bound. Even in this life there tend to be positive consequences for keeping God's laws. But the negative, downward powers are still at work, pulling us in the opposite direction. Even for those who live saintly lives, temptation and sin are still at work, seeking to pull down and tear apart and lead to destruction.

This means that even those who are already Christians need to be on guard against disobedience to God's laws. Sin does not lose it's power to destroy; it is still a force to take seriously even for those who have overcome it with God's help. In short, the only things that help us get off the ground are God's law and his mercy. If we ever turn our back on those forces in our life, sin still has its power to pull us down. Sin is a force never to be forgotten; even when we have overcome the power of sin through Christ, sin still leads to death. To follow Christ and be obedient to him leads to life. One force tears you down. The other lifts you up. Soar!

Let us pray:
Lord, open our eyes to the ways in which we have sinned against you or our neighbor, by thought, word, action, or lack of action. Forgive us and restore us to be the people you intend for us to be, so that we may follow your ways, which lead to abundant and everlasting life. Amen.

SUGGESTED PSALM: *Psalm 11*

SUGGESTED HYMNS:

"I Sing the Almighty Power of God" (B, E, P, UM, W)

"God of Grace and God of Glory" (B, C, E, F, L, P, UM)

Facing Consequences

Hearing the Word

One reason that today's devotional scripture (Psalm 16:5-11) was selected to go along with the lesson scripture (Jeremiah 6) is because both contain references to choosing the right path in life. Jeremiah says, "Stand at the crossroads . . ." He counsels his original listeners, apparently unsuccessfully, to look for the good way and walk in it. Likewise, Psalm 16:11 says, "You will show me the path that leads to life. . . ." The idea of walking on the right path was a common image in the Bible. Cars hadn't been invented, and people choose the right path to get to their destination, much like we follow signs along a road to know which road will lead us to wherever we want to go.

Living the Word

In the old Road Runner cartoon, Wily Coyote loved to change the road signs in an effort to fool the Road Runner. A typical example would be to change a sign at a fork in a road. Let's say the right-hand fork is the "right way," and the left-hand fork leads to a cliff. Coyote would move the sign from the right-hand fork to the left-hand fork. Then, to prevent the Coyote from realizing it had been fooled by seeing the drop-off up ahead, that tricky rascal would make a huge mural of a road winding peacefully through the hills and place the mural at the edge of the cliff. That way, the Road Runner would think it was running down the road, but instead run through the mural and fall off the cliff.

Somehow, the Road Runner, in spite of his "bird brain," managed to overcome such challenges. It was as though the writers of the cartoon were determined to protect him even if he accidentally made the wrong decision. If he crashed through the mural and fell off the cliff, he would land on Coyote's head. This would not only punish Coyote for his evil plan, but also break the Road Runner's fall and save him from becoming a finger-linking good dinner.

The psalmist says, "My future is in your hands. . . . I praise the Lord, because he guides me, and in the night my conscience warns me. . . . You will show me the path that leads to life . . ." (Psalm 16:5, 7, 11).

Some paths in life lead to destruction. They may be destructive to you, or to others, or perhaps on a communal level to the community or our environment. For example, excessive drinking can lead to bodily illness or death. It can destroy job opportunities, relationships with family and friends, and so on. On a communal level, it makes a difference to the amount of coal that is burned and greenhouse gases cast into the atmosphere whether everyone decides to conserve electricity or everyone decides to ignore the pleas of atmospheric scientists. Just as certainly, other paths lead to life, to joy, and to the good things God wants to give us in life. For example, treating other people the way we want to be treated tends to win friends and preserve the love of family more than fighting bitterly with others over petty issues.

While our lives are not determined to the extent of having only one right choice to make, God is willing to help us determine the difference between right and wrong, and help guide us when we stand at a crossroads in our life.

Many people wonder how to "hear" God's voice in such times. Certainly it is good, on a practical level, to pray, to seek the advice of others who have walked a similar path, and to mentally "try on" different choices to see which one(s) "feel" like you can make them with joy and with a clear conscience. The psalmist speaks of our conscience warning us when we are considering something that is wrong; further, the psalmist seems to equate our "conscience" to the nearness of God's presence. The more we seek to listen to the difference between right and wrong, which is really like trying to listen to God, the sharper our "hearing" will become.

Let us pray:
Lord, please help guide those who must make important decisions in this week. Speak to us all, that in the small, seemingly insignificant choices between right and wrong we may consistently choose the right paths that we might not wander away from you an inch at a time. Amen.

14

  "Praise to the Lord, the Almighty" (B, E, F, L, P, UM, W)
  "O Master, Let Me Walk with Thee" (B, C, E, F, L, P, UM)

Listen Carefully

Hearing the Word

Proverbs is a collection of short sayings and other wisdom writings. Even though it contains some theological ideas, it is mainly practical advice. The theology behind it closely parallels the idea behind Jeremiah's prophecy (from today's lesson scripture); both hold the basic belief that God will punish evil people, and righteous people will be rewarded. Therefore, the prophet's role of warning the people to turn from their sins is often accompanied by what seem to be threats. The teaching found in Proverbs 4 is written as though it is a father talking to his child, but behind the words the idea is still clear that to obey the teachings of wisdom is to be rewarded, but to disobey is to head for trouble.

Living the Word

A Sunday school teacher asked her class whether one of the Ten Commandments teaches us about how to treat our parents. One bright child raised her hand and said, "Yes, there is. 'Honor thy father and mother.' " "That's right!" exclaimed the teacher. "And is there one that teaches us how to treat our brothers and sisters?" The same little girl raised her hand again, and answered, "Thou shalt not kill."

In the teaching from Proverbs 4:20-27, there is an interesting progression of thought. First the writer cautions, "Be careful how you think; your life is shaped by your thoughts." After considering the importance of our thoughts, next his instruction deals with speech: "Never say anything that isn't true." A short time later, he warns his youthful listeners about actions: "Plan carefully what you do. . . . Avoid evil and walk straight ahead. Don't go one step off the right way."

15

Thoughts lead to words and deeds. Sometimes we say that we "speak (or act) before we think." But even when words and actions are spontaneous knee-jerk reactions, they still occur against the backdrop of all our earlier thoughts, beliefs, attitudes, habits, and values. For example, it is more likely that someone who speaks or thinks using colorful language will scream out a swear word if startled, while someone who systematically seeks to eliminate that kind of language is less likely to respond to a sudden scare in the same way.

Therefore, to control our thoughts is essential if we are to control our words and deeds. The issue is far more important than whether or not a person swears when startled. This writing in Proverbs points out that the way we think paves the way for everything else in our life. If we honor God with our thoughts, if we respect other people with our thoughts, if we cultivate wholesome and loving thoughts about others, then we are more likely to speak and act in those ways. On the other hand, if we secretly think sarcastic thoughts about our boss, it will not be long before one of them slips out and we will regret it! "Be careful how you think; your life is shaped by your thoughts."

All of this means that Christians have a special challenge; not just acting like a Christian, but trying to be one in the inner self, in the privacy of our thoughts. There is no need there for pretension. We can dress up and look sophisticated whether or not we are, and if we are not it might fool some people. But there are only two who truly know your real thoughts—you and God, and you can't fool either one of them.

The good news about our faith is that it is transforming from the inside out. In Romans 12:2, Paul writes, "Do not conform yourselves to the standards of this world, but let God transform you inwardly by a complete change of your mind." Therefore, the conventional wisdom of our faith is more than just acting like a caring and loving person; it is to become one! Then once we think, and are, that way, we will naturally act like it.

Let us pray:
Lord, help us tame our thoughts, and bring them under your control. And then, like a refreshing river that flows from a pure spring, we will be able to speak and live in such a way that you are honored, and our neighbor is served with love. Through Christ we pray. Amen.

16

Justice Demanded

Hearing the Word

In his letter to the Ephesians, Paul uses the image of light and darkness to illustrate the difference between a life that is lost and a life illuminated by the spirit of God. He spells out the moral implications of a life lived in the light. In a sense, he is like the prophet Jeremiah. Both were speaking to an audience that presumed itself to be religious, and yet had failed to fully apply its faith to the real issues of justice and moral living in their current situations. Jeremiah (the subject of the lesson scripture for today) noted that the leaders and people had placed more trust in gaining prosperity than in seeking true justice in their land. Likewise, Paul was clearly interested in helping his church at Ephesus discard their old values and take on the new values that following Christ demands.

Living the Word

George Burns was once quoted as saying, "When you stop giving and offering something to the rest of the world, it's time to turn out the lights." His thought makes a good point. When a person comes in to work in the morning, the first thing they do is turn on the lights. When they are ready to quit for the day, they turn the lights off as they leave. The "work" he implies we should be doing is to give and offer something to the rest of the world.

As a way to look at life, that's close to what Paul is saying to the Ephesians: "Make good use of every opportunity you have. . . . Don't be fools, then, but try to find out what the Lord wants you to do" (5:16-17).

Someone who was in charge of his church's mission fund once said, "I have some good news and some bad news. The good news is that we have enough money to completely pay for our new mis-

17

sions campaign. The bad news is that it is still in your checkbooks."

There are too many ways in which the good things that could be done in the world by the church are left undone. But I suspect that in every church there are more hours of work given in every week to tinkering with personal and church finances than there are given to mission work and local service. How many hours would you guess are spent by your pastor and members of your congregation in an average month balancing the checkbook, looking at budgets at home and/or church, searching for a better interest rate on a used-car loan or refinancing a home mortgage? Down at the local discount homebuilding store you can hardly find a shopping cart on a Saturday because of all the people looking for a good deal for lumber for a new deck around the swimming pool. What if for just one Saturday a month, they all swung a hammer down at a local Habitat for Humanity house instead?

There are so many opportunities! Consider tutoring an at-risk child in the school, or trying to make a difference in the neighborhoods in the cities where most of your church families lock the car doors when they drive through. Suppose that every Christian family in America with multiple cars earnestly sought a way to do with one less auto, and then gave the savings to world hunger. How many American Christians would die as a result of this inconvenience, and how many hungry children wouldn't? Maybe that's too radical of a thought—or is it? We have many opportunities, large and small, to give something to the world. Too often we settle for the small ones, like the man who looked in his wallet as the offering plates were about to be passed in church. There was a one-dollar bill and a twenty. He struggled a moment, then remembered the sermon, "The Lord loves a cheerful giver." So he grabbed the one-dollar bill and thought, "I'll be a lot more cheerful about giving this."

The more we put our faith to work, and seek the opportunities to do God's work in this world, the longer the lights need to be on. For we will be busy down at the church until this old world is just the way God really wants it to be.

Let us pray:
Lord, you have surrounded us with opportunities to put our faith to work. Open our eyes to see them, and our hearts to give ourselves to them. Amen.

READ IN YOUR BIBLE: *Hebrews 10:11-18*   October 20, 2002

SUGGESTED PSALM: *Psalm 51:1-10*

SUGGESTED HYMNS:

"*More Love to Thee, O Christ*" *(B, C, F, P, UM)*

"*There's a Wideness in God's Mercy*" *(All)*

Hope to the Weary

Hearing the Word

Just as Congress occasionally changes the tax laws, today's scriptures deal with a change in the Law. However, the change God is making is more significant and sweeping than any Congress might ever boast of making. In Hebrews 10, the writer (who may be Paul, but most scholars question who wrote it) explains this change in the Law by quoting from the Old Testament prophet Jeremiah (which is the source of today's lesson scripture). As Jeremiah explains it, the Law is no longer an external set of rules, but an internal set of values and directives. Instead of grumbling while the Law is kept, people will know in their heart what is right, and want to be obedient. The old system of rules, adds the writer of Hebrews, involved making sacrifices to atone for sins, but Jesus' coming was another sweeping change in the rules; his death atoned at once for all the sins of the world.

Living the Word

After a fishing trip, I told the congregation in a sermon about one of the fish I caught. As fishermen are prone to do, I indicated the length of the fish by holding my hands apart.

During this same time, the church had a pen-pal program going. Participants were given a mystery friend, but we didn't know who was writing us letters each week. All I knew about my mystery friend was that it was a child.

The week after I told my "fish story," I received a tape measure and note from my mystery friend that said, "Use this tape measure in your fishing box. Now when you show the church how big your fish was you don't have to use your hands. Use the tape measure."

I thought it was both funny and cute. I kept the note, and if I

19

catch a really huge fish, I'll use the tape measure (smaller ones are easier to "estimate"!). However, my mystery friend's gift does fundamentally change the rules for a fisherman who likes to brag about the big ones. It substitutes the rule of scientific proof for the long-accepted notion that fishermen fish all day. Then they come home, and make up lies. In short, by giving me a tape measure, my mystery friend turned the rules of fishy storytelling upside down.

The writer of Hebrews is talking about a radical change of the rules, except instead of measuring fish these rules are about how you and I measure up.

For a moment let's consider the philosophy behind animal sacrifice. In Old Testament times, it was thought that an offense against God (namely sin) required a penalty fee, much like speeding today results in a ticket. In the case of sin against God, the penalty cannot be paid with money; it must be paid with a different kind of currency—life itself. Since God gives the privilege of life, expecting us to "spend" it well; thus the penalty for disobedience is the loss of life. Since most people don't want literally to give up their own life, the idea behind the sacrifice of animals was to transfer the sins of the person onto the innocent animal, and then make it pay the price of the person's sin. One problem with this system was that the sacrifices continually had to be made, since people continued to sin. But Jesus offered himself as a perfect sacrifice, effective for everyone and effective forever.

No longer, then, do we have to look in a mirror and wonder how our lives measure up to each and every commandment. We can even be pretty sure we fall far short of the commandments. Gone are the days for creative exaggeration, vainly trying to convince God and others that we are a notch or two better than if we pulled out the tape measure of the commandments. Instead, we all know that we do not measure up to the perfect life portrayed in the commandments, but Jesus does measure up. And he has turned the old rules upside down. You don't have to brag anymore, or make up lies. For in God's kingdom they use the measure of Christ, and so we are all keepers.

Let us pray:
Lord, thank you for your love and mercy that you have shown to us through our Lord, Jesus Christ, an innocent and good man who willingly gave his life even for sinners. Amen.

READ IN YOUR BIBLE: *Hebrews 11:32–12:2*   **October 27, 2002**

SUGGESTED PSALM: *Psalm 78:1-7*

SUGGESTED HYMNS:

  "Be Thou My Vision" (B, E, F, P, UM)

  "O God, Our Help in Ages Past" (All)

Faith Overrides Despair

Hearing the Word

Have you ever been discouraged about something, and had someone try to encourage you by telling you about people who have made it when they have been in your situation? The audience of Hebrews 11:32–12:2 apparently faced persecution for their faith. To encourage them, the writer goes into great detail about the "crowd of witnesses" who have gone before them, and stood firm in their faith. Their life and witness should inspire us and encourage us to persevere in our struggles. Habakkuk may have lived in Old Testament times, but he was also facing a time of persecution (the Babylonian exile, close to the end of the seventh century B.C.). Like the writer of Hebrews, he drew inspiration from the stories of the faithful from years past, and hoped that God would continue to show himself in the present day.

Living the Word

At a track meet, watching youth run relay races is almost a theological event. As each runner finishes his/her leg of the race, that runner must pass a metal baton to the next runner who carries it to the next runner, and so on. In this way, all four runners function as a single team. Interestingly, the team that wins may not be the team with the four fastest runners in the competition. The winners could be the team who does the best job passing the baton.

When the baton is about to be passed, the receiving runner does not stand still. He/she begins to run, looking ahead, but with one arm stretched back to receive the baton. If the receiving runner takes off too fast, he/she may outrun their tired teammate, and then lose the race because the baton was not passed.

21

So the ideal is to run, eyes straight ahead, but without forgetting that you are receiving and building on the performance of those who have been running before you. This, it seems to me, is an important picture of the Christian life for today's church.

Many churches focus on their past. They get so wrapped up in tradition and history that it would seem criminal to change it. "We can't do that . . . it has never been done that way before." To resist change, to resist forging ahead into uncharted waters is to build a house in the desert instead of moving ahead while we keep alive the dream of the promised land. It is true we must move in step with our past, and know it well. We must know it well enough that we don't have to focus on it. Remember: The best runners don't look back. They know exactly when the baton is about to be placed in their hand without having to look back. Instead, they look ahead and focus on getting to the finish line.

Sometimes we want to make changes that are two sweeping, too aggressive. If a church suddenly throws away all the hymnals and puts the words to the songs up on the wall, always uses a band instead of the organ, never prints a bulletin anymore, and doesn't even keep any of the familiar liturgy, then it is really not even the same church anymore. There will be people in that congregation who feel lost, like the next runner has no interest in the baton they have been carrying all of their life. Certainly there are ways to weave together the old songs with the new technologies, and sing the new songs on the old organ. Tradition has a vital part in the life of the church; it gives us a foundation on which to build, and a record of achievement to encourage us in the hard times.

The challenge in the church today is to blend rock music and the good, old hymns, tennis shoes and ties, ice-cream socials and the Internet. It is a good time to keep our eyes forward, fixed on Jesus, young and old, and to keep our hand stretched behind us to receive that faith and encouragement that is vital to help us win the race.

Let us pray:

Lord, in these days of such rapid change and sometimes strong resistance to change, help us know how to run the race of our hectic lives, eyes fixed on you. In Jesus' name we pray together, young generation and old generation, as one team with you. Amen.

READ IN YOUR BIBLE: *Psalm 75*   **November 3, 2002**
SUGGESTED PSALM: *Psalm 53*
SUGGESTED HYMNS:
  "Amazing Grace" (All)
  "Jesus, the Very Thought of Thee" (B, E, F, L, P, UM)

Facing the End

Hearing the Word

One concept that deserves more of our consideration is the idea of God's judgment, particularly his final judgment. Psalm 75 speaks of God's judgment. It is linked to the lesson scripture for today (2 Chronicles 36:11-21) because it is about how God brought judgment upon Israel for their disobedience and their disregard of God and God's prophets. Their punishment seemed final (it was the Babylonian exile), but even that catastrophic ending led to another new beginning in the time of Ezra and Nehemiah.

Living the Word

When a criminal seems to escape justice in the courts, it is not unusual to hear victims console themselves with the thought, "They avoided paying for their crime here on earth, but someday they will have to answer to God." This comment anticipates that God will deal harshly with the criminal in the afterlife, and perhaps throw the person in hell.

Having been a victim of a crime (a kidnapping and robbery at gunpoint when I was a teen), I have complete sympathy for crime victims. I also feel that I can understand the desire to see the person who has victimized you receive punishment. However, as a Christian and a minister, I wonder whether we can truly expect God to deliver the appropriate level of anguish, physical torment, or even eternal punishment to people who have hurt us. I'm not saying we cannot count on God for justice—I am saying that some parts of the Bible paint a picture of a God who not only has justice, but who also has mercy.

A story on television recently profiled the case of a man who, in a drug-induced moment of his youth, killed a young woman. The murder case went unsolved for years, then decades. Meanwhile, this killer who escaped justice turned his life around, got married, had a nice family, and became a pillar of his church. Eventually he decided to confess his crime and turn himself in, and that's what made it an unusual story. But suppose he had not. Suppose he just went on living his life, going to church, taking communion next to people whose sins were more like gossip and lies and maybe even a few worse things thrown in. Would God forgive them, but not the killer? As a minister, I would have to say that God would forgive the killer too.

Now, perhaps God's final judgment will be different for those escaped killers (and other sinners) who are unrepentant; after all, the man in the example above had turned away from his sin, and to his credit, even voluntarily gave himself up to receive his earthly justice when it was clear he never would have had to do so. But should we as Christians actually hope that criminals who escape earthly justice will NOT ever repent so we can feel more hopeful that God will refuse mercy to them?

It is difficult to remember, but important, that God's overall hope for us is that we will be reconciled with him and with one another. Therefore, even punishment as seemingly final as having the promised land taken over by the Babylonians and the Temple wrecked turned out to be a learning process, a desperate last-ditch way of seeking a renewed relationship with the people.

Could God really hope that the infamous mass murderers of our day can be emotionally and spiritually restored to wholeness? Could God really be hoping that if they were, by some long shot, admitted into heaven, that any of us would be willing to sit across from them at the lunch table and talk to them in peace?

I guess God hopes a lot. But if anyone has the power to judge, the power to forgive and the power to renew, then surely it is God.

Let us pray:

Lord, we recognize that you have the power to judge, and the right to condemn any of us for our sins. Forgive us, we pray, and teach us what it means to have the kind of hope and mercy you must have for others. In the name of Jesus, who prayed that even his killers might be forgiven. Amen.

READ IN YOUR BIBLE: *Psalm 42:5-11*   **November 10, 2002**

SUGGESTED PSALM: *Psalm 137*

SUGGESTED HYMNS:

"How Great Thou Art" (B, F, L, P, UM)

"A Mighty Fortress Is Our God" (All)

Hope Born Out of Despair

Hearing the Word

Jeremiah is known as the "weeping prophet" because of the book of Lamentations (which he is thought to have written, and which is placed in the Bible right after the book of Jeremiah). He was weeping as he wrote the five poems of Lamentations because of the destruction of Jerusalem in 586 B.C. (during the Babylonian exile). Psalm 42:5-11 is written as a prayer, but it also comments on the Exile in poetic fashion. Note that Psalm 43 continues the "Prayer of a someone in exile" (see, for example, the "refrain" linking the two psalms which is repeated in verses Psalm 42:5, 42:11, and 43:5). Even though the event was a crushing, and seemingly final blow to the existence of the Israelites as God's people, the lesson and devotional scripture for today include a theme of hope even in the midst of their justifiable despair.

Living the Word

In the hard-to-believe-it-is-true category: A man, in a parking lot, came across a woman holding a baby who was obviously upset. When he asked her what was wrong, she exclaimed, "I'm locked out of my car!" Then, thrusting the car's remote control door-locking device at him, she complained, "This little push button thingy must have a dead battery because it won't unlock the doors!"

Taking the remote control device from her, he noticed that it was dangling from her keychain. He asked, "Do any of these keys go to the car?"

"Yes, the one with the black plastic will start the car, but the problem is I can't get inside to start it with a dead battery in the remote."

25

With that, the man opened the door with the ignition key. "Here," he said. "You're going to have to use the key to get in the door until you can get a new battery for your remote."

As I reflect about Psalm 42, it seems to me to be the story of someone who is locked out of the promised land, and yet who holds the key in his hand. It is the moving and earnest prayer of a man in exile, which, if you think about it, is almost an oxymoron. After all, why were the Israelites in exile in the first place? It is because they did not turn to God. They forgot to pray, or did so without any sincerity or feeling. They did not turn to God or bother to place their trust in him. Instead, they put their trust in other places. So in this heartfelt prayer, in simply turning to God in this time of despair, the healing and renewal has already begun. In wishing to go back to the promised land in the form of a sincere prayer to God, it is like thinking the door is hopelessly locked when really the key is in your hand all along.

There are many frustrating and difficult situations in our lives, including divorce, addiction, abuse, mental turmoil, physical pain, financial problems, family problems, work problems, and grief. When we encounter problems, it is easy to think of one solution only, or even to be able to imagine none.

However, the psalmist continues, "I will put my hope in God, and once again I will praise him, my savior and my God." Even when we are in situations where our ability to imagine solutions has run out, God is never out of possibilities. This does not mean that we only have to pray, and every trouble will easily go away— far from it! However, it does mean that God is a "key" resource to help us through life's most trying and difficult times.

So if you ever feel as though you have run out of options, and your problem has "about got you licked," remember that you have one more powerful resource in your hands. In fact, prayer is asking God for help, for a fresh perspective, and to stay with you until you can find a solution.

Let us pray:
Lord, be with those who feel distressed or lost or in grief today. Particularly be with those who feel they have exhausted every resource and come up empty-handed. Instead, help them draw near to you, and come to know that no sad burden or evil situation can defeat your awesome ability to help us through. Amen.

26

READ IN YOUR BIBLE: *Romans 6:17-23*   **November 17, 2002**
SUGGESTED PSALM: *Psalm 128*
SUGGESTED HYMNS:
 "This Is My Father's World" (B, C, E, F, L, P, UM)
 "How Firm a Foundation" (All)

Transformation Required

Hearing the Word

In the days of Ezekiel, many Israelites thought that sins would necessarily result in negative consequences in this life. Further, since children were an extension of the self, it was not unreasonable to them to think that their sins might result in punishment falling on their children. For example, the accidental death of a child might be understood as punishment for a sin of the parent. Through Ezekiel, however, God challenged that belief. Ezekiel said that each person would be held accountable for his/her own sins, and further, that individuals had a chance to repent and avoid the punishment that would otherwise be coming to them for their sins. Today's devotional reading, found in Romans 6:17-23, echoes the belief in individual accountability that has become an important theme of our Judeo-Christian heritage.

Living the Word

A friend told me he saw a large snapping turtle, seemingly exhausted, laying in the middle of the hot pavement of a county highway. He stopped his car along the shoulder of the road and walked back to put it safely on the other side. Moments later he noticed a big truck coming, so he began to jog toward the turtle. Right away it was clear he did not have time to get to the turtle before the truck would be dangerously close. As he waited by the side of the road for the truck to pass, the truck driver made a spiteful face at my friend, actually crossed the centerline, lined up his tires with the turtle, and smashed it right in front of him.

The two men in the story had completely different intentions as they approached the turtle. One meant to save it, and the other meant to kill it. My friend had compassion in his heart, but the truck driver had no mercy. In my friend's effort, you can catch a glimpse of God's nature at work, and you can see the destructiveness of evil at work in the cruel act of that truck driver.

Both forces are real in today's world. As we look around us at the lives of people, there are marriages torn apart by alcohol, addiction, lust, adultery, and greed. Children are sometimes beaten and even killed by the very people who should love them. Every day money is stolen from the helpless, and people are raped or shot or stabbed. Evil is a genuine force at work in our world. Sin leads to death and destruction of all kinds. The apostle Paul points out that we can live our lives as slaves of evil if we choose to do so. And many do.

On the other hand, you can also see God at work in the world. When a person decides to give four times what they did last year to world hunger, when a person says yes to a lowly task just to help someone in need, when a person shows patience and kindness to someone who isn't deserving of it, when one person forgives another, when someone gradually recovers from grief with the help of a loving community, you can see God at work. The apostle Paul points out that we can live our lives serving God's good purposes if we choose to do so. And many do.

But no matter which side we decide to serve, the basic story of our life is much like the story of the turtle on the road. We have wandered from God's perfect will, and as a result, we are in the path of destruction. Helpless to save ourselves, God has made a run for it in an attempt to snatch us from the jaws of death. In the case of the turtle, unfortunately the truck was faster than my friend, and it spelled disaster for the turtle. But in our life story, the good news is that God gets there first!

God is willing and able to rescue us from the path of evil. We must simply place ourselves in God's hands, the one who loves us and wants the best for us. The one to serve is God, who even gave his life to save ours.

Let us pray:
Lord, like a turtle carried to safety by a caring person, we cannot begin to understand your love and grace. But help us show our thankfulness with a life that is pleasing to you, and lived in service to you. Through Christ, amen.

SUGGESTED PSALM: *Psalm 41:1-20*
SUGGESTED HYMNS:
　"My Hope Is Built" *(B, C, F, L, P, UM)*
　"Rejoice, the Lord Is King" *(B, E, F, L, P, UM, W)*

Change of Heart

Hearing the Word

The mighty Babylonian army was gathering outside, and anyone could see that they were making preparations to attack. And anyone could see that they would be conquerors and take anything they wanted. Against this background, real estate values drop in a hurry. There are a lot of sellers, but nobody wants to buy land that is about to be taken over by invaders. Strangely, Jeremiah, at the Lord's direction, publicly bought a field in this setting. His purchase was a powerful sermon designed to let the people know that he, God's spokesperson, expected to be able to return to the land someday, and that the time would come when the people would honor God and live as God's people in the promised land once again.

Living the Word

One of the more amusing letters I have read was written by Martin Van Buren to President Jackson on January 31, 1829.

To President Jackson:
　The canal system of this country is being threatened by the spread of a new form of transportation known as "railroads." The federal government must preserve the canals for the following reasons:
　1. If the canal boats are supplanted by railroads, serious unemployment will result. Captains, cooks, drivers, hostlers, repairment, and lock tenders will be left without means of livelihood, not to mention the numerous farmers now employed in growing hay for horses....
　As you may well know, Mr. President, the "railroad car-

riages" are pulled at the enormous speed of fifteen miles per hour by "engines" which endanger the life and limb of passengers, roar and snort their way through the countryside, setting fire to crops, scaring the livestock and frightening women and children. The Almighty never intended that people should travel at such breakneck speed.

It is difficult for any of us to see beyond the limits of our present situation. If we have never known trains, then we cannot appreciate the improvements they might bring. This same thing happens in church meetings. If someone suggests the benefits of a computer for the church office, for example, it is easy for opponents to argue, "We've never needed one before, and therefore we don't need one now. It would be a waste of money, and a source of technological problems. In fact, it would probably turn kids to drugs, encourage crime in the church, and even break up many happy marriages."

Too often we see "what is" and not "what could be." It takes faith and hope to see "what could be." You can't see it with your eyes. You can only see it with your heart, with a creative vision, and with prayer. Jeremiah was such a visionary. When everyone in Jerusalem was focused on the Babylonians amassing for an attack outside of the city walls, he saw an opportunity to buy land cheap! More than that, of course, he saw that the future was still in God's hands. He could see that the "what could be" included the people returning to faith in God, and consequently, returning to the promised land.

As we count our blessings in this season, the "what is" includes staggering world hunger, the suffering of refugees from war, the homeless in our cities, the ravages of poverty here and abroad, the tendency to look for military solutions for peace instead of seeking understanding. But the world needs more than people who look at "what is," and complain about it. The world needs people of faith and hope, who look at "what could be," and work with God to make those visions come true.

Let us pray:
   Lord, open my eyes to see more than what is; help me see what, with your love and help, could be. Then grant me the strength and determination to work with you to bring about a new reality that is more just, more peaceful, more hopeful, and more loving. Through Christ, amen.

READ IN YOUR BIBLE: *Isaiah 40:3-11*   December 1, 2002
SUGGESTED PSALM: *Psalm 47*
SUGGESTED HYMNS:
  "O Come, O Come, Emmanuel" (B, E, F, L, P, UM, W)
  "Joy to the World" (All)

Rewards of Faithfulness

Hearing the Word

Isaiah 40 marks a complete change of tone in the prophet Isaiah's message. It is much like the change in voice from an angry parent who sends a disobedient child to time-out, only later to go into the time-out room to comfort the weeping child. In Isaiah 1–39, the prophet was warning the people of Israel that if they didn't change, then they would be punished. In between Isaiah 39 and 40, the punishment came in the form of the Babylonian army, casting the people of Israel into exile in a foreign land. In this setting, Isaiah seeks to give the exiles the gift of hope for a brighter future. He does so by painting a picture of the road that they will follow to get back home again.

Living the Word

During this season, many college students come home for Christmas break. Seeing them brings back memories of what it was like to come home after being away at college. After being away for a long time, everything is familiar and relaxing and welcoming when you come through the front door of your long-time home. Often part of homecoming is the smell of a special dinner being prepared, and a hug at the front door, and happy greetings. You may have been away for a long time, but like Dorothy said in the *Wizard of Oz*, "There's no place like home."

Christmas is a lot like coming home. But if it is a homecoming, then let's consider why we have been away.

Do you remember the Albanian refugees who fled for their lives from the invading Serbian soldiers? They were stripped of their possessions and kicked out of their homes. Many of them, especially the men, were shot and killed. Then, as the war for the "homeland" continued, the refugees had to live in terrible conditions. All they wanted to do was get home again.

The people that God spoke to through the prophet Isaiah were in a similar predicament. The Jewish people had been kicked out of the promised land by the Babylonian army in the year 586 B.C. Like the refugees from Kosovo, they wanted to go back home.

Our sins are like a powerful army that attacks us and kicks us out of our rightful home, like the Albanian people of Kosovo who were forced out by the Serbs; or the Jewish people who centuries ago were evicted from their promised land; or like Adam and Eve who were ousted from paradise because of their disobedience. Our sins lead to our eviction, to our separation from God. Sometimes we are kicked out, other times we wander away in boredom or forgetfulness or busyness. We may turn away in rebellion, or slink away in shame. No matter how it happens that we leave home, we are not "at home" because it's hard, impossible really, to sin and still look God straight in the eye. That's why this scripture brings all of us good news: Jesus came into the world to bring us "back home," to help us be "right at home" with God.

It is easy to get swept away with all the other ways of "preparing" for Christmas. If you ask, "Are you ready for Christmas," most people will respond by telling you whether they have completed their Christmas shopping. Or the question will bring to mind Christmas card lists or cookies to bake or outside decorations that should have been put up while it was still nice weather! But another vital way to "get ready for Christmas" is to pray, worship, and try to eliminate barriers between God and us. This is a good time to get to church more often. If there is someone you have a grudge against, it is a good season to forgive and seek reconciliation. It is a good time to reflect on our life, ask what God would have us do, and make some new commitments.

Because of Jesus, the front door is open wide after such a long absence, and we can feel the familiar, accepting love of being at home with our God.

Let us pray:
Lord, help us be prepared not only for the Christmas holiday festivities, but for you to come into our heart, into our life, and into our world. Amen.

SUGGESTED HYMNS:

"Angels We Have Heard on High" (B, E, F, L, P, UM, W)

"It Came Upon the Midnight Clear" (All)

Accepting the Call

Hearing the Word

Psalm 146, which is today's devotional scripture, matches the theme of praise for God that is found in Mary's song of praise. (Her song of praise, voiced after the angel let her know she would bear the Son of God, is known as the "Magnificat." The Magnificat comprises the last eleven verses of today's lesson scripture found in Luke 1:26-56.) Psalm 146 also expresses many of the expectations found in scripture for the Messiah, in particular those in the passage that Jesus selected to identify the purpose of his ministry (see Isaiah 61:1-3). These include giving food to the hungry, setting the prisoners free, giving sight to the blind, lifting those who have fallen, and helping widows and orphans.

Living the Word

I received a powerful single word sermon from a one-year-old. After a worship service, I was greeting parishioners as they left the church. A little girl toddled up to me, pulled her hand out of her mouth, and pointed at me with her wet finger. Then, with a big grin on her face, she said, "Jesus!" People nearby laughed. I don't know whether they laughed because that little girl was so cute, or because she had just made such a far-fetched comparison!

Anyway, her mother quickly explained that they had been reading religious books at home, and talking about how Jesus was at church. I have a beard; and in the picture books, her mother noted, Jesus has a beard too. So her daughter jumped to the conclusion that the bearded guy at church must be Jesus.

Aside from the fact that she was a cute child saying something funny, I have to tell you it is a weird feeling for someone to look at

33

you and think you are Jesus. Right away I wanted to shake my head and say, "No, I'm not Jesus. I'm just Jeff."

When someone calls you "Jesus," it brings to mind the contrast between Jesus and yourself—for most of us, the "different from Jesus" list is longer than the "similar to Jesus" list. Take, for example, these three things: Jesus was sinless, perfect, and not even grumpy when someone asked him about the subject of income taxes. (How do you rate on that last one?)

Psalm 146:3-4 warns us, "Don't put your trust in human leaders; no human being can save you. When they die, they return to the dust."

Sometimes people outside of the church expect too much of pastors and church members—and I think many church members expect too much of their fellow members, too. It is because, like this little girl, they confuse us with Jesus, and so they're disappointed by our imperfections; disillusioned if our sins show. After all, to point a finger at us and say we are Jesus is simply a mistake! We are the ones God made from the dust. We are mortals and sinners. Only Jesus is the perfect one.

That doesn't mean we can flippantly excuse ourselves as sinners, and forget about trying to be like Jesus. The same Psalm talks about the work of God, and much of it sounds like the work we should embody as Christians. Among other things, God "gives food to the hungry . . . sets the prisoners free and gives sight to the blind. He lifts those who have fallen. He protects the strangers who live in our land; he helps widows and orphans." In other words, the work of God is exactly the kind of work God wants to do through us!

It is haunting to think of those innocent little eyes looking at me, a sinner, and expecting me to be like Jesus! If the hopeful eyes of a child don't motivate a person to try to live a better example, what will? Her little finger pointed at me made me hope that as she grows up, she will somehow see Jesus at work in my life.

How about you? After all, people in the pews next to you, and in the world, are watching you too, and hoping to see Jesus in you. The eyes of the world, and of little children, are on you too.

Let us pray:
Lord, may we live up to your name as you seek to carry on your work through our lives. Bless the children, and save us from ever disappointing them as they seek to see you living in us. Amen.

34

SUGGESTED PSALM: *Psalm 24*

SUGGESTED HYMNS:

  "Hark! The Herald Angels Sing" (All)
  "O Come, All Ye Faithful" (All)

Obedient Living

Hearing the Word

As the Jewish people looked back at their history, King David stood out for them much like many churches can look back and remember with longing an abundant time under the leadership of a loved and particularly effective pastor. Therefore, it seemed only natural, as they looked for a Messiah to come, to expect that the Messiah would be a descendant of King David. Isaiah is expressing this hope and expectation, along with God's dream of what the Kingdom would be like under the Messiah's leadership. This devotional scripture is linked today with the lesson scripture found in Matthew 1:18-25, the story of the birth of Jesus. It also mentions that Joseph, Jesus' earthly father, was a descendant of King David.

Living the Word

Have you ever thought of something ideal, and said to yourself, "Now, that's the way things should be"? Isaiah 11 is a vision like that. It was probably written during a time that was not ideal or peaceful—that's why the vision is of an ideal leader and a peaceful kingdom. To show how peaceful things are, Isaiah's vision even includes a description of animals that are traditional enemies now getting along.

In our home, we have a dog and four house cats too. Usually the cats (wisely) avoid the dog, who doesn't have good manners toward the cats. One day one of the cats came tearing up the steps to the kitchen while we ate breakfast. The dog happened to be standing at the top of the steps, sideways, completely blocking the stairway. Apparently the cat did not look ahead very well, or maybe when cats are on a tear they don't. Anyway, by the time it realized that it was traveling at full speed and only a couple of feet from the dog, it didn't have long to think about its options (like going around the dog or jumping over it). In a snap decision that surprised us and certainly surprised the dog, it scrambled between the dog's stomach and the floor, like running under a bridge. You'd have to know our dog, I guess, but that certainly violated her space. It would normally have been an act of war, except that no war resulted. The cat kept right on running, as if it had planned all along to rocket underneath the dog on the linoleum. And the dog, once it got over the shock, simply went back to watching us eat breakfast. No creature did so much as snarl or bare a fang or even hiss. For one brief moment, it was as though friendship and understanding and tolerance had broken out in the animal kingdom, right in our kitchen!

Think of all the things that keep people apart, or make them enemies. One person owes another person money, but can't pay it back. Two married people discover that they are better at fighting than forgiving. Racial attitudes, economic inequalities, border disputes, and even whether or not to cut back on the church budget can set one person against another. Nearly every day in the news we read about one country or faction or political party or protest group that is attacking another. And will Cardinal fans ever get along with Cub fans?

Isaiah's vision of a perfect, peaceful kingdom seems impossible in a world full of people who seem bent on war, who sue each other over ridiculous things, and who even curse at a stranger for "cutting them off" on the highway. This vision of God's perfect kingdom, as impossible as it seems, is still important. It gives us a perfect pattern to look at while we are measuring our own lives, and a high goal to strive for.

Let us pray:

Lord, fill my life with your peace, the peace that comes from knowing and following Christ. Give me the strength of character to respond with kindness and understanding to those who irritate me and even those I might consider as enemies. Help me become better at forgiving, and not worry so much about winning an argument or proving myself in the right. Help me live in peace with all people I meet each day through putting your love and forgiveness into practice in my daily life. In the name of Jesus, our perfect vision and the prince of peace. Amen.

A Wondrous Birth

Hearing the Word

Isaiah 9:1-7 contains some of the most beloved words of the Bible: "The people who walked in darkness have seen a great light." However, the end of chapter 8 and the first verse of chapter 9 are read less often. They portray a discouraged and hungry people, wandering through the land seeing nothing but a deep and terrible darkness everywhere they look. It is against this backdrop of suffering that these words, written to the people who walk in darkness, have particular meaning. When this scripture is paired with today's lesson scripture (Luke 2:1-20), then it is interesting to notice that Jesus' birth, which occurs at night, is marked by a beautiful star in the sky.

Living the Word

On May 10, 1994, Central Illinois and other parts of the United States experienced an eclipse of the sun (during which the moon passes between the sun and the earth). This was a rare event; it will not occur here again until September 14, 2099! Students all across the area were instructed in advance about how to view the eclipse safely, and allowed to go outside to watch it at about noon that day. They constructed special viewing boxes or wore specially made glasses to protect their eyes from the 11 percent of the sun's face that was not covered during the height of the eclipse. During the time when the sun's surface was most hidden, the darkness over the earth was similar to about a half hour after sunset.

In a way, the eclipse of the sun was the opposite of today's scripture, "The people who walked in darkness have seen a great light. They lived in a land of shadows, but now light is shining on them." The darkness didn't even last quite four minutes, but it was memorable. You could say that it made us look at the sun "in a whole different light." Those moments of darkness made us appreciate the sun's light, and realize how much we depend on it. Though it was just a brief moment in time, it is one that had a powerful effect. It would be a little like losing all your possessions, even just for a few minutes, and then finding them all again. Even though you got them back, you had a few minutes to think about how you would feel if they were suddenly gone.

When Jesus was born, there was a strange and beautiful star in the sky. It gave an unusual light that led some star-watchers to Bethlehem, and caused them to think that it indicated the birth of a king. Even though that night did not last long, it changed their lives, and the lives of countless others, forever.

When Jesus was born, he came at night. That is a powerful symbol. He comes to people who are used to darkness; not just the absence of light, but the presence of heartache, problems, trouble, and sin. His birth was not in an antiseptic hospital, but out with the poor and outcast, with those who get no recognition or notice. He was born at night, to a people whose eyes are used to the darkness. Quite often, the darkness is what we expect from life.

But God noticed us! The light came to the people who walk in darkness! Jesus was born to humble commoners, not to royalty. Outsiders noticed the light of his coming, as did some shepherds who had to work third shift. The people who walked in darkness, who are used to it, were given a life-changing glimpse of the light of God.

You never forget it if you have seen the sun's light covered in darkness at noon, if even for a few moments. Those few moments make you look at sunlight in a different way. In the same way, I suppose you'd never forget it if you saw the light of God pierce the darkness of life, if even for a moment. I guess it would change the way we look at darkness forever, wouldn't it? Has the glimpse of light revealed in Jesus Christ changed the way you look at the darkness of this world? It can, and it should!

Let us pray:
Lord, thank you for sending your son, Jesus Christ, into the darkest, most threatening corners of our lives, so that we may see your light, have hope, and share the good news of his birth with all the world. In Christ's name, amen.

   "Fairest Lord Jesus" (B, C, E, F, P, UM)
   "Infant Holy, Infant Lowly" (B, F, L, P, UM, W)

Preparing the Way

Hearing the Word

John 1:1-14 is filled with themes of light versus darkness to sym-
bolize those who worship God as seen in Christ versus those who
reject him. It also speaks, in poetic fashion, about the ministry of
John the Baptist who is supposed to prepare the way for Christ's
ministry. The lesson scripture for today (Matthew 3 and 11) also
describes the role of John the Baptist as the person who prophets
foretold would prepare the way for Christ. He did so by preaching
in the desert, confronting people of their sins, and baptizing them.
Both passages also are careful to differentiate between the role of
John and Jesus. John was the one whose life pointed the way to the
light, and Jesus came to be the light of the world.

Living the Word

I love to be part of a candlelit Christmas Eve worship service. It
is beautiful to see all those people holding candles, preparing to be
bearers of Christ's light in the world.

Someone once said that it is better to light one candle than to
curse the darkness. In response to the world's problems, God sent
a baby named Jesus. It was a simple act, much like lighting a single candle. God could have sent an army to enforce good conduct,
but instead sent a child to teach and inspire us. Just as a single
candle casts light over an entire dark room, the life of one person,
Jesus, casts a light on all the darkness of the world.

One of the special moments in the Christmas Eve service is
watching people pass the light throughout the crowd. One person
gives the gift of light to a neighbor whose candle is dark and cold.
But it is not like a gift that, when given, leaves the giver with less.
Instead, after the light is shared, both candles glow. When we

"light a candle" in the world, the act of sharing it simply multiplies the glow.

Whether or not you attended candlelit Christmas Eve worship, the most important and beautiful part of that symbolic service actually takes place now, as we look ahead at a new year of life. How can we as individuals light a candle in today's world in our daily life? Here are a few ideas:

- Try to be available for a friend who is worried or struggling with emotional pain. Maybe it is a phone call or a loaf of bread with a note or a hug, but to help someone know he or she is not alone is a day-brightening thing to do!
- Visit a nursing home, and pause to exchange some friendly small talk with someone there you do not know.
- If you are married, surprise your spouse with a flower, a note, a special meal, or a ticket to his or her favorite event. Practice an extra level of patience with the things you don't like, and rise to a higher level of kindness in the things you do for your spouse.
- Watch for every opportunity to pat a child or youth on the back and give him or her a sincere compliment, a hug, or some other gesture of love and support.
- Try to be a person who succeeds in drawing out a youth in conversation; try to be an excellent, involved, supportive, and caring listener.
- Look out for someone who is alone or lonely, and sit next to him or her. Talk a while, maybe even issue an invitation to get together later.
- Take a moment to share your faith with another person. It could be something simple like "I believe in prayer, and I'll pray for you," or "I know it's difficult right now, but I still believe God will find a way through this," or "I have found it challenges and encourages me to go to church. Would you like to come with me Sunday?"

Let us pray:
Lord, may we receive with joy the light of your love and freely share it with others. For you have come into the world, not to be hidden under a bushel of busy schedules and misplaced priorities, but shared so that others may see and believe. In Jesus' name we pray. Amen.

SUGGESTED PSALM: *Psalm 49*

SUGGESTED HYMNS:

"*My Hope Is Built*" *(B, C, F, L, P, UM)*

"*How Firm a Foundation*" *(All)*

Setting Right Priorities

Hearing the Word

Paul wrote two letters to Timothy that are included in our New Testament. He may have written others too, but would not have always needed to write him, as Timothy was a companion and helper for Paul through at least part of Paul's ministry. Timothy was younger than Paul, and Paul uses this letter to instruct Timothy about the Christian faith and to warn him about false teachings. The portion selected for our devotional reading today focuses on the perils of trusting in riches. This is in keeping with the theme of the lesson scripture today, and was one of Jesus' regular subjects too.

Living the Word

A man kept his money carefully hidden in a hole in the ground. The hole was under a giant oak tree at the end of an old stone fence. Each day the man would visit the spot. Crouching in the shade of the tree, he would dig up his money and carefully count it. Then he would put it back into the ground and cover it up again. One day he decided to show his fortune to a friend. When they arrived at the tree, the man saw that his fortune was gone—only a hole in the ground and a pile of dirt remained. "I've been robbed!" he exclaimed in grief. "My fortune—it's gone!"

"That's terrible!" said his friend. "What were you doing with it?"

"I didn't do anything with it," the man replied. "I just liked to come here every day and look at it."

"Well then," the wise friend remarked, "you really haven't lost anything. After all, you can still come here every day and look at the hole in the ground. It will do you the same amount of good."

41

Paul observes, "What did we bring into the world? Nothing! What can we take out of the world? Nothing!" (1 Timothy 6:7). Whatever we earn or possess will eventually be in someone else's hands, someone else's control, and someone else's bank account. We can postpone all the decisions about our money until after we die, but if we do, then other people will make all the decisions for us. If we are never robbed in this life, death will come along and rob us of the chance to decide, to put our assets to work for the Lord. Even if we carefully stipulate in our will who will get which possessions and who will receive what percentage of our money, then if we wait for the will to be executed, we will personally receive none of the joy of giving. There is obviously the need to make smart choices between current needs, future needs, and benevolent giving. But do we have to wait until we're dead to be generous? Won't the Lord still provide for us if we are alive and generous?

Paul encouraged those who are rich in the things of this life to "do good, be rich in good works, to be generous and ready to share with others" (1 Timothy 6:18). Riches represent a tool. The power that money represents can be wasted by lack of a decision, by endlessly putting off a way to put it to work. Churches are notorious for doing that with memorial funds. The money given in memory of loved ones comes in ten and twenty dollars at a time, and the church accumulates it. Month after month goes by with no discussion about the memorial fund. So the money builds up, a pile of potential good going unused. How big is your church's memorial fund? Is it just a fortune sitting in a hole in the ground? Are there any new church starts in your area that desperately need the money if your church is rich enough not to be able to figure out how to use it?

Then give another long, hard thought to your own financial plans. If you have anything sitting in a hole in the ground, don't be foolish. Be wise, and a good steward. Ask God to help you be courageous enough to make a decision about what to do with it. Remember, unused, it doesn't matter if you have a million dollars or a hole in the ground—it will do the same amount of good.

Let us pray:
Lord, you have been generous to us in many ways. Make us wise stewards of all you have given us that we may do the maximum amount of good in the world while we live and serve you. Amen.

SUGGESTED PSALM: *Psalm 91*

SUGGESTED HYMNS:

"Lord, Speak to Me" (B, C, F, L, P, UM)

"'Come, We That Love the Lord" (B, C, E, F, UM, W)

Purposeful Friendships

Hearing the Word

John's Gospel, unlike Matthew's, Mark's, and Luke's, contains more lengthy and deep theological statements by Jesus to his disciples. The other Gospels tend to quote Jesus as telling parables that are light on theological expounding, and using short, memorable statements such as "The first shall be last, and the last shall be first." Today's reading from John 15 is part of a long and beloved speech of Jesus to his disciples. In this section, he speaks of his love for the disciples, and reminds them that he chose them for their task. His primary point is to command them to love one another in the same way that he has loved them. The fact that Jesus chose his disciples links this text with the lesson texts for the day (selections from Luke and John), because the lesson texts reveal the close and purposeful friendship Jesus had with Mary, Martha, and Lazarus.

Living the Word

One of the most common conversations salespeople have with shoppers, from shoe stores to used-car lots, goes like this:

Salesperson: "Hi! May I help you find something today?"

Shopper: "No, thanks. I'm not buying anything today—I'm just looking."

Now, any salesperson who has been on the job very long knows that the shopper may sincerely believe what he or she just said, but on the other hand, the shopper did not fall out of a plane and accidentally land on the used-car lot. They may not have found the used car they want to buy yet, but, on the other hand, they are looking because they have already made a decision on some level to buy a used car.

This is worth mentioning because in our Christian faith, we often stress the fact that we have chosen to be Christians. "I heard a really great sermon at a revival, and I decided to follow Christ," one person might say. Another person might say, "I had never gone to church much, until my neighbor invited me to go to church camp when I was in high school. And for some strange reason, I went. And after that, I became a Christian."

Our relationship with God is, ideally, a two-way matter. God loves us, and hopefully we love God too. The debate over infant baptism is a case in point. Some churches baptize infants because, they say, it stresses the fact that God's love and acceptance is already there before we can do anything to earn it or deserve it. Infant baptism makes the point that all of our deeds, and even decisions, are merely responses to the already-present love of God. On the other hand, those who support believers baptism for adults only argue that baptism is a sign of a person becoming a believer, and how can an infant, who cannot even say the word "God," be a believer? So representatives on both sides agree that this love for God and this love from God are both necessary—they just disagree about which part of the relationship baptism should celebrate.

Still, Jesus makes an interesting comment here in John: "You did not choose me; I chose you and appointed you to go and bear much fruit" (15:16). It sounds as if God has a purpose for us, even before we realize it or have a chance to accept it. An important and meaningful part of God's love for us is the realization that we never would have had the chance to choose God, or to decide to follow Jesus, if God did not already love us enough to give us the opportunity, and tug our hearts in that direction.

It may be a simple thought, but it is somehow reassuring to think that God was not passive, like a used car sitting on a lot, rusting away until we discovered God. Rather, God is the one who went out shopping, looking for the ones beside the road, forgotten on the lot, and listed in fine print in the paper. God really wanted to look for us, and he found us, and he chose us.

Let us pray:
Lord, thank you that before we ever knew you or had a chance to make a decision about following you, you already had your eye on us, and wanted us to belong to you. May we rejoice in your love, and share it with others! Amen.

Truth and Character

Hearing the Word

When you read the devotional scripture lesson (encouraging Christians to respect and pray for civil leaders) alongside the lesson scripture for today (about Pilate deciding to let Jesus be crucified), it feels a little uncomfortable! Christianity has always had a strange relationship to the government through the centuries; the early church, from which Paul is writing, was persecuted from time to time in various areas. About three hundred years later the church became the civil authority, which created a different set of problems. In any case, Paul's advice here is for Christians to pray for kings and others in authority, showing he had no intention of overthrowing the government; instead he was expressing his mission to seek to bring all people, including leaders, to Christ.

Living the Word

Many churches have two flags on the altar. One is the American flag, and the other the Christian flag. One flag represents our loyalty to this earthly kingdom we call the United States of America. The other represents our loyalty to our heavenly kingdom. Because of one, we pay taxes and may serve in the armed forces. In exchange we benefit from the various services the government provides.

The other kingdom has no geographical territory, and no system of taxation. Its laws govern our values and behavior. It is not an earthly kingdom, but it has lasted and will last far longer than any earthly kingdom. God's kingdom is not normally in conflict with our earthly loyalties, but we need to be aware that the possibility exists, and know how to manage those conflicts.

First, it is always possible that the laws and implementation of

45

our country's laws could violate, or at least not be in keeping with, the values of God's kingdom. We therefore should evaluate all present and proposed new laws through a different set of criteria than the general public might. For example, when tax cuts are discussed, there may be a tendency for those in elected office to structure tax relief to include favorable treatment for their wealthy benefactors rather than the poor, who cannot contribute to their re-election fund. This may be legal in America, but don't forget that other loyalty we have. Who will speak up for the poor, if not the citizens of God's kingdom?

It is still true that the majority of people on death row managed to get there partly because they had poorer legal representation than the rich can afford. These days numerous people are being exonerated by DNA evidence, but they spent time in prison because they had poor legal counsel. The legal system is our nation's way of expressing and implementing justice. It seems that citizens of God's kingdom should be interested and involved in talking about justice, reconciliation, fair punishment, and the rehabilitation of human beings.

This date is close to Martin Luther King Jr. Day. He knew the conflict that can exist between loyalties to both flags. He spoke, marched, endured beatings, and even went to jail to protest unjust laws in our land. In so doing he made our country a more just place; but he also stood up for the kingdom of God.

It is good to pray for those who lead our country, and to carefully consider the proposals, laws, policies, and problems they face. They need the involvement of well-informed citizens of both kingdoms. Sometimes they need our support, and sometimes they need to be challenged and opposed by us. This is one way God can use us to strengthen God's kingdom here on earth. Those two flags represent two great dreams, both worth our allegiance. One nation with liberty and justice for all—but a nation under God, which is motivated by and compared to the perfect dream of God's kingdom of love, justice, and peace.

Let us pray:

Lord, make us effective citizens of our nation. Strengthen our nation and your eternal kingdom. Help us know when our loyalties are in conflict, and be courageous enough to put you first. May your kingdom come, and your will be done, on earth as it is in heaven. Amen.

READ IN YOUR BIBLE: *Acts 4:1-13*   **January 26, 2003**
SUGGESTED PSALM: *Psalm 80*
SUGGESTED HYMNS:
  "Take Up Thy Cross" (B, E, L, P, UM, W)
  "Guide Me, O Thou Great Jehovah" (B, C, E, F, P, UM)

Failure and Restoration

Hearing the Word

The lesson scripture for today deals with two important parts of Peter's relationship with Jesus. The first part was his three-time denial that he even knew Jesus. In spite of the fact that only hours before he swore to Jesus that he would never deny him, and in spite of the fact that Jesus had clearly identified Peter as the person who would become the new leader once Jesus died, Peter still denied that he knew who Jesus was. After the Resurrection, Jesus appeared to Peter and three times asked Peter if he loved him. Three times Peter affirmed that he did, and each time Jesus told him to take care of his flock. This is commonly known as the "reinstatement" of Peter (necessary because of the earlier denials). The devotional scripture from Acts shows a moment when it would have been easy for Peter to deny knowing Jesus, since Peter was under arrest and in "hot water." But instead he was bold in proclaiming his faith, showing him to be the great leader Jesus had originally expected him to be.

Living the Word

The cover of major news magazines often feature people who have made big mistakes in their lives. One week it may be the story of a financial executive caught embezzling millions of dollars from his clients. The next week it could be a story about a woman who, in the midst of postpartum depression, killed all her children.

What happens to these people when their story is no longer in the news magazines? Do they move to another country and change their names? How do they pick up the pieces when major mistakes or sins shatter their lives? And is it even possible to go on after such an incident?

One wonders how many stories there are in the lives of ordinary human beings that feature really big mistakes. Just think about all the shattered marriages caused by adultery, or all of the unmarried mothers who realized too late that they will have to raise their child as a teenager, alone, without any support from the child's father. In fact, human life without a major scar is probably the unusual thing.

Peter is an inspiration for those who think they have messed up their life, for those who feel there is no way to recover and go on with life. Peter was a beloved disciple who was destined to become the next leader for the church after Jesus. Then he made the terrible mistake during the last days of Jesus' life of denying that he even knew Jesus. It says in the Bible that he wept bitterly, and you can believe it. In his mind, that failure made his resignation mandatory and immediate.

That is why it is so refreshing to know that Jesus made a point to approach Peter after the Resurrection and give Peter a chance to redeem himself and carry on. Jesus didn't want even a catastrophic failure to stop his beloved disciples from serving him.

We all sin and fall short of God's plans for us. Sometimes that sin seems minor and even invisible to others. Sometimes it is major, costly, and even newsworthy. But the Lord is just as forgiving, just as anxious to help us move forward. That's what God invented the rest of your life for!

Jesus built his whole church on the man who had a record of denying him. He didn't fire him or even bawl him out. Jesus looks at every one of us, no matter what our sin, no matter how severe our mistakes have been, with an eye for making the rest of our life a wonderful story of recovery and usefulness in God's kingdom. There is no mistake or sin in your past that will keep God from wanting to be reunited with you. Don't let any shame, any prison cell, any big mistake from the past stop you, for God is still with you, and nothing can stop God!

Let us pray:
Lord, help us trust in your redeeming work, especially when we or someone we know are faced with sins or mistakes that seems too major to recover from easily. Remind us that you are the God who made a great leader out of a man too afraid to admit he even knew you, and you can bring new hope and new purposes to any of us, no matter what our circumstances. Amen.

Encouraging Others

Hearing the Word

The point of Hebrews 10:19-25 is that through Christ, we can approach God directly. We no longer need the mediation of a priest to go behind a curtain to a sacred place to pray on our behalf. The curtain referred to was in the innermost sacred part of the Temple, where the high priest would go to offer sacrifices on behalf of the people out of their view. The writer of Hebrews also wanted Christians to gather regularly to worship together, as this would be a source of encouragement in their faith. It is this theme of encouraging one another that links this passage to the lesson scripture for today (selections from Acts), which focuses on Barnabas, who was an encouraging person.

Living the Word

One thing most churches are missing is a team of cheerleaders. Cheerleaders show up to sports events and encourage their home team. One good thing about cheerleaders is that they never seem to get discouraged. Their team can be down 100-0 with two seconds left, but until the final buzzer sounds, they will still be cheering on the sidelines. Giving up and pouting is just not in their nature!

Why can't we have cheerleaders come to church? But instead of sending a team of young, lively cheerleaders—into a place where people's problems can be far more serious and threatening than a bad game—we send a person we've trained by making them write long papers about ecclesiology! (A parishioner's comment: "I've never seen my preacher's eyes. During his prayers he closes his, and during his sermons, he closes mine.") Nothing against preachers (I'm one), but some of us focus more on content than on enthusiasm. Many of us are the opposites of a cheerleading

49

squad—they leap into the air, we kneel on the floor; they shout, we pray in stained glass tones; they are young and thin, we—well, never mind.

Encouragement and enthusiasm tend to build on each other. What would happen in your church if, after you heard a good point in the sermon, you shouted "Amen!" I can tell you that most preachers would be shocked, not because it is unwelcome to know that someone out there listened and had a positive reaction, but because that kind of affirmation is unusual in many churches. Churches used to be built with an "amen corner," a place near the front where people were actually supposed to shout "amen" and otherwise encourage the preacher.

It is a good thing, though, for laypersons to express strong support, verbally to their pastor and to others about their pastor. Focus on the good qualities in your pastor and be free about complimenting those things. Forget about the disappointing characteristics. If you hope some other pastor won't be as disappointing, then realize that the secret isn't finding a superhuman pastor. Remember that none could ever be without disappointments, and that it is far better instead to focus on the qualities you appreciate. Then work to encourage and build up those good gifts, and the church will be stronger. The more you criticize and discourage, the weaker your pastor's leadership will be, and your church too. Encourage your pastor, and soon he or she will want to return the favor by saying good and uplifting things to you.

By the way, this same principle applies to every workplace, and to every family group. Christians should be people who habitually look for the good, who refuse to let go of hope, who seek to build up other people. The writer of Hebrews wanted us to gather at church to encourage one another, but it is also a good thing to be an encourager wherever we go. You can do it, and if you don't know how, go to a sports event. Watch the cheerleaders. Let them make you smile and look at the bright side; let them help you figure out a way to support the team, and how to encourage others.

Let us pray:
Lord, I know that it feels good to have other people encourage me. Therefore, whether I receive that from others or not, help me be that kind of person for everyone I meet—my family, my pastor, my friends, and even for strangers who just need an uplifting word. Through Christ, amen.

SUGGESTED PSALM: *Psalm 131*
SUGGESTED HYMNS:
"Lord, I Want to Be a Christian" (B, C, F, P, UM)
"Hope of the World" (E, L, P, UM, W)

Obeying the Call

Hearing the Word

Paul is in prison when he writes this letter to the church at Ephesus. His main theme in this part of the letter is that Christ has created unity between Jews and Gentiles (non-Jews, including the people at Ephesus, who were not Jewish) by bringing a plan of salvation that transcended the Jewish laws and covenant community. In many of his letters, he seems to feel the need to shore up his authority by reminding the readers of who he is and how he has worked on their behalf. This is important because it is easy to imagine that in his lengthy absences, and in the presence of teachers who willingly or unknowingly teach false doctrines, his authority would often come under question. Here he does not miss the opportunity to let them know he is in prison on their behalf, and he reminds them of his story on the road to Damascus (from which he also derives authority, as that was the direct command of Christ to Paul). This same story appears as part of his testimony before King Agrippa in Acts, today's lesson scripture.

Living the Word

I remember a story about a man who was waiting to board an airplane when the announcement came that the flight was delayed. Immediately he jumped up and angrily confronted the booking agent. "I demand to be reseated on another flight!" he fumed in a voice everyone in the area could hear.

The booking agent attempted to explain that it would take time to find him another flight, and that she could not guarantee him a seat with another airline. The man continued to fume and bluster and make impossible demands as she tried in vain to help him.

Coming up empty-handed, the agent said, "I'm sorry, sir, but I simply cannot find another flight for you this evening."

The man slammed his hand on the counter, leaned across, and shouted, "Do you know who I am?"

At that, the booking agent grabbed her microphone and announced, "Attention passengers. We have a problem. The man at the counter says that he does not know who he is. Is there anyone here who can help this man?"

The experience that Paul had on the road to Damascus must have made an incredible impact on his self-image. He regularly refers to the story in his writings, and it is certain that he would have retold it in his preaching. The question of "Who am I" for Paul was completely redefined by that experience of meeting Christ on the road to Damascus. As evidence that it completely changed his self-image, his name even changed from Saul to Paul.

If you had to tell someone who you were, and what your life's purpose is, what would you tell them? How do you define yourself? You don't have to answer this question out loud, but surely you have some idea. Consider the following two responses: "I'm the father of three sons named John, Bartholomew, and Daniel, who are ages 4, 6, and 9 . . . and by the way, I also play professional baseball," or "I'm a pro baseball player. My batting average is .367 in 289 times at bat, and I have a good shot at a Golden Glove Award. And oh, by the way, I have three kids, all sons."

Sometimes particular events in life help shape who we think we are. Circumstances can change us into a plane crash survivor, a crusader for cancer research, a married person, a single person, a parent, an unemployed person, or perhaps a TV weather forecaster.

Like Paul, meeting Christ is one thing that should completely reshape our understanding of who we are. Because of knowing Christ, we are forgiven instead of sinners, we are on a mission instead of chasing the wind, we are beloved children of God instead of people who must struggle to prove our self-worth to a world that judges worth by productivity and the almighty dollar. In Christ, we are new people! That's who we are!

Let us pray:
Lord, thank you for making us new and forgiven people. Help us live out our identity as your beloved children by loving others and serving you with joy. Through Christ, amen.

READ IN YOUR BIBLE: *2 Timothy 2:1-7*   **February 16, 2003**

SUGGESTED PSALM: *Psalm 143*

SUGGESTED HYMNS:

  "Abide with Me" (B, C, E, F, L, P, UM)

  "Holy, Holy, Holy" (All)

Playing a Supportive Role

Hearing the Word

Paul's second letter to Timothy is to encourage him to carry on his work as Paul's assistant and representative, in spite of Timothy's suffering and the opposition of others. Paul himself is in prison at the time, and if you read the rest of the letter, you get the strong feeling that Paul has truly been hurt by the desertion and opposition of various people who he once trusted. He is genuinely grateful that Timothy has continued to be a source of support for him; in the lesson scriptures for this day Paul compares his relationship to Timothy to a father/son relationship, one where there is not only love but also a shared mission in life.

Living the Word

A man was driving down the highway when his car phone rang. He answered, and it was his wife calling. Her voice was anxious and worried.

"Herbert, are you on Highway 75?"

"Yes, I am," he replied. "Why?"

"Well, please watch out then! The news guy in the traffic helicopter said that there is a problem on Highway 75. I got worried because I figured you might be on that road right about now."

"I am," he said. "What's the problem?"

"There is a car going the wrong way down the highway."

Herbert replied, "Oh, it's a mess, all right! But it's not just one car going the wrong way—it's hundreds of them!"

Paul's second letter to Timothy reminds me of that story. It's a good thing Paul and Timothy didn't have cell phones, or we wouldn't have a written record of Paul's thoughts. He apparently felt like he was traveling down the highway, and everyone else was going in the wrong direction. Not only was he in prison, but he was also hearing of people who abandoned him, opposed him, and even violently threatened him. But Timothy was like a breath of fresh air. He was a supportive and hard worker, willing to carry Paul's message to others and go where Paul asked him to go. He trusted Timothy to bring his possessions to him, to carry messages for him, and in short be his trusted assistant.

Being an assistant pastor is one of the more difficult roles to play—it is much easier, in some ways, to be the senior pastor of a staff than one of the associates. That's because associates are often fresh out of seminary. They are full of their own ideas, which they have been dreaming up for years. Then when they finally get out there into the church, they find that their senior pastor has ideas and expects the associate to help implement and carry out those ideas. Some senior pastors genuinely share leadership with their associates. More often, being an associate means that you have to concentrate on the ideas and plans of another person, or perhaps a larger staff, and carry out those plans.

We might look at our Christian lives as being God's assistants. The work we are carrying out is really not our own—it is God's. God's plan has been made and communicated, and now God needs people to assist in carrying out that plan. The more we are willing to set aside our ideas, when they are different from God's will, the more effective we will be. The more we can trust God to know the best direction for us to go, and be faithful and available to work, like Timothy was, the more God can do through us.

Sometimes it may seem like we are in a crazy world, where everybody is going the opposite direction from us, but that is not a surprise. God's plan is not like the plans many people in the world have made for themselves. So when we do God's will, we are often going against the prevailing current. But God is with us on our way. Just as Paul loved Timothy like a son, so God's love for us is strong. Let us serve him with all that we are.

Let us pray:
Lord, help us know when to put aside our plans, and know when you want us to change directions for you. Give us the courage we need to assist you in your holy plans for this world, that we may be effective servants in your hands. Amen.

Partnering in Mission

Hearing the Word

Ephesians includes an overarching theme of the unity found in Christ, particularly the unity between those who were Jews and those who were Gentiles. In the later part of the letter, Paul wants his readers to put their common faith and unity into practice in ways that are visible in their daily lives. Once again, Paul reminds his readers that he is a prisoner, just as he did one chapter earlier. It seems to have the effect of saying, "Since I am going through this on your behalf, surely you can do this one little thing for me." Paul was excellent at arguing persuasively and utilizing any point he could to convince his readers to do what they should do.

Living the Word

The History Channel featured a presentation by Roger Mudd called "One Hour Over Tokyo: The Doolittle Raid." It was the fascinating story of the United States' response to the bombing of Pearl Harbor. On April 18, 1942, our country sent eighty men in sixteen bombers, led by flying ace Jimmy Doolittle, to launch a surprise attack on the Japanese mainland. The large planes had never been launched from an aircraft carrier before, so Doolittle spent weeks training the volunteers how to get the lumbering planes airborne in just 450 feet! It was known to be a one-way trip over Japan before landing in a friendly part of China.

Because the aircraft carrier was detected four hundred miles short of their anticipated take-off point, they launched the planes hours early. This meant they had to land at night in China instead of during daylight hours, and it placed their fuel supply in grave doubt. They successfully attacked Japan, but none of the planes

55

were able to land safely in China. Eight of the men who jumped that night landed in Japanese territory. All of them had to undergo prolonged torture in dark, solitary confinement. Three were executed. The other five, including one man named Jacob DeShazer, were kept as prisoners until the war ended some forty months later.

Jacob DeShazer was given a Bible. He memorized as much of it as he could, and let it sink in, including the part about loving your enemies. His faith, which had been a part of his life only in a nominal way before the war, suddenly became real and strong. He asked God to help him change the hatred he felt for his captors to love, in spite of their continued cruel treatment. Gradually his attitude became friendly and positive.

When the war ended Jacob felt called to become a minister. Amazingly he returned to Japan as a missionary and evangelist! Meanwhile a written account about how Jacob had forgiven his captors had been published and spread among the now-hurting Japanese people. This helped create opportunities for Jacob to preach in Japan. His ministry continued for more than thirty years, resulting in the conversion of many people and the start of more than twenty new churches!

One highlight of his ministry was the conversion of Mitsuo Fuchida; he was the Japanese pilot who had led the raid on Pearl Harbor. After reading the account about how Jacob had forgiven his captors, Mitsuo purchased a Bible, read it, and accepted Christ! He went on to become an evangelist too! The two former pilots had been among the first to bomb each other's homeland, yet now they were friends, working together for Christ!

If we allow Christ to do so, he can bring unity even to the most divided situations (yes, even between you and the stubborn person you just thought of as an exception). If the Lord could bring together these two former enemies, and make them friends and coworkers for the Lord, then surely the Lord can heal all of the divisions, grudges, and hostilities we hold in our heart too!

Let us pray:
Lord, help us forgive, and seek true reconciliation with those who have hurt us in any way. Melt away the walls that divide us, so that we may live in unity with one another, brought together as brothers and sisters in your precious name. Amen.

SUGGESTED PSALM: *Psalm 34*
SUGGESTED HYMNS:
  "Take My Life and Let It Be" (B, C, E, L, P, UM, W)
  "He Leadeth Me: O Blessed Thought" (B, C, F, L, UM)

The Beginning of the Gospel

Hearing the Word

The lesson scriptures are beginning a two-month series that provide a run-through of Jesus' life from the beginning of his public ministry through his death and resurrection. Therefore, the lesson scripture for today, from Mark 1, covers Jesus' baptism, temptation, first sermon, calling his first disciples, and first healing. The devotional scripture, found in Luke 4:14-21, focuses on Jesus' sermon and subsequent rejection in his hometown of Nazareth, based on his reading of Isaiah 61:1-3. In Luke's Gospel, as in Matthew's, this event also follows Jesus' baptism and temptation in the wilderness. Unlike Mark, Luke and Matthew include Jesus' birth stories and trace his lineage to David (and Luke goes back all the way to Adam) as a way of setting the stage for Jesus' public ministry; Mark begins telling Jesus' story when Jesus is already an adult.

Living the Word

A pastor preaching his first sermon in his first church was quite nervous, and he forgot his second point. He remembered the advice of his preaching professor, who said, "If you ever get stuck in a sermon, don't admit that you've forgotten. Instead, simply repeat your previous point."

The previous point had been Jesus saying, "Behold, I am coming soon." So the new preacher took his professor's advice and repeated the statement, but it didn't help. So this time he said, more loudly and with feeling, "Behold, I am coming soon!" This didn't work either, so finally he flung himself at the pulpit and shouted at the top of his lungs, "Behold, I am coming soon!"

Unfortunately, it was an old church, and termites had been working on the floorboards about where the pulpit stood. When his body hit the pulpit the old boards gave way, and the pulpit toppled forward. The pastor tumbled right over the top of it and landed in a heap in the lap of a woman who was sitting in the front row.

"I'm sorry," he stammered, not knowing what to say. But she interrupted him. "No, pastor, it's my fault. I should have gotten out of your way—you told me three times you were coming."

Jesus' first sermon was nearly as eventful, except the people were not quite so forgiving. They grabbed him and planned to throw him off a cliff. But he did succeed in getting his first point across. He announced the mission statement for his life and ministry. He read the words of the prophet Isaiah found in 61:1-3, and then told the people that those scriptures were being fulfilled in his life. They were pretty impressed by that part, considering they knew him as a local carpenter and a kid who had grown up in their synagogue. But when he got to the second point, the one about God taking care of the non-Jewish people too, he got kicked out of the synagogue. They believed the part about the Lord coming to save his people, but Jesus included everyone in the God's people part, and did not limit it to the Israelites.

Jesus felt his life was fulfilling the scriptural purpose of saving the people. He did this by giving his life for us, but he also did this through concrete acts of love and assistance that we can carry on. As he did, we can notice the poor and lonely, the social outcasts, the sick, and the needy. Like he did, we can invite people to give up their sin and follow Christ. As he did, we can seek to love everyone, including our enemies.

I'm not sure what the second point was going to be of the pastor's first sermon. But maybe a good second point to the "I am coming soon" sermon would be "and we are coming for a holy purpose—to do God's will and carry on Christ's work in the world."

Let us pray:
Lord, help us learn more about Jesus and his ministry. Help us carry on the work of love and service that he preached to us and showed us in his daily life. Amen.

SUGGESTED PSALM: *Psalm 40:1-11*
SUGGESTED HYMNS:
  "Savior, Like a Shepherd Lead Us" (B, C, E, F, L, P, UM)
  "My Shepherd Will Supply My Need" (B, E, F, P, W)

Jesus Calls Sinners

Hearing the Word

This week the scripture readings have a twin theme. First, there is already the theme of a developing conflict with the Jewish leaders (scribes and Pharisees). Second, there is a clear theme that Jesus has come to minister to the lost and outcast of society. In the lesson scripture, there was such a crowd around him that the man he forgave and healed had to be lowered through a hole made in the roof! In the devotional reading, from Luke 15, Jesus essentially shares his reasoning for his interest in the lost by telling the story of the single lost sheep. The reason he felt compelled to explain himself, however, was because of the criticism and hostility of the Pharisees and teachers of the Law toward Jesus' welcoming outcasts and even eating with them.

Living the Word

One comedian wondered aloud why they put locks on the doors of stores that are open twenty-four hours a day. His question does point out an inconsistency, doesn't it? They say they are open twenty-four hours a day, always available and convenient, and yet they must also be planning, at least at some future time, to be unavailable and closed!

The same question could be asked of the church. When we lock the doors, who are we locking out, and why must it be that way?

Of course, there are good practical reasons for locking the church, but it points out a deeper, more troubling fact. We, as a church, have still not eliminated being exclusive, choosing the people we want to let in and the ones we want to keep out. The most powerful evidence is simply looking around any given church on Sunday morning, see who's missing from that community, and see what the people in that church are doing about it.

Consider the following: Does your church give baskets of food away at Thanksgiving or Christmas? If so, do the people who receive them come to your church through the rest of the year? Do you know their names and the names of their children, the particular challenges that they are facing, or whether they go to other churches? Too many of our churches are in middle- and upper-income neighborhoods and "reach down" to help people on public aid. This makes the wealthier people feel good about doing something, but there is not enough continuing ministry, and the people on the Christmas basket list don't get invited to our Sunday school parties or vacation Bible school.

Do you see what I'm getting at here? I believe that Jesus would spend more time talking to the huge crowd of rowdy teens we complain about because they make noise on Saturday night and leave their beer cans in the parking lot, or talking to the people who we watch to see if they're going to steal from our store again. He even went to their parties, and ate with sinners! Then when people like us, faithful church folk, criticized him for ignoring we who are the good supporters, he told the story of the concern the good shepherd has for the one sheep that is missing from the flock. That shepherd would leave the other ninety-nine and go searching, diligently looking, and fully intending to bring back the lost sheep. The good shepherd didn't come back after ten minutes and blame the lost sheep, as we do in a thousand different ways: "Well, I tried! If that sheep wants to be part of the flock, it will have to make more of an effort to be found! The trouble with one missing sheep is that it is easy to miss unless you are pretty diligent about noticing, and pretty determined to bring it in.

It makes me uncomfortable to write this devotion because it convicts me about some people I know. If reading this has made you uncomfortable too, then it may be God telling you that yes, there is someone missing from your flock in your town too.

Let us pray:
Lord, open our eyes to see the lost who live right around us, and open our hearts to imagine them sitting next to us in church, growing closer to you, and growing in fellowship with a loving community of believers. And that which we have imagined, help us work for you. Amen.

The Power of Jesus

Hearing the Word

If Jesus was God walking on the earth in human form, then it is easy to accept that he had tremendous power available to him, as God would. Today's devotional scripture demonstrates that power in the form of healing a man who, for years, had been unable to be healed in any other way. The lesson scripture picks up the same theme of the power of Jesus through the story of Jesus calming the storm at sea. This feat amazed the disciples, who saw, in a man who could calm the wind and waves with a command, the power of God at work in Jesus. While this incident did not cause any friction with the Pharisees, who were not there to see it, the healing of the man by the pool (in the devotional reading) did cause problems. The reason is because the healing happened on the Sabbath; but probably more so because they felt confused and even threatened by a person who claimed to be the Son of God and who could demonstrate such miraculous power.

Living the Word

A parishioner told me a story about a scientist who said to God, "Human beings do not need you any more. We scientists can heal people of virtually every disease, and even make exact clones of any person we want to duplicate." The scientist went on to explain how far science had advanced, and pointed out that any miracle in the Bible could now be explained away by scientists.

God listened carefully, but did not seem concerned. When the scientist was done talking, God said, "OK, if you want to prove it, I'll challenge you to a person-making contest." The scientist accepted.

God said, "I'll make my first person just the way I made Adam.

Let's see if you can do that." So God bent down, grabbed a little bit of soil and held it tenderly in the palm of his hand. Suddenly a new person appeared, already fully clothed, who stood right next to God, put his hands on his hips, and immediately spoke to the scientist on God's behalf, "Look at me! God just made me from the dirt! Let's see you do that!"

"That's no problem," the scientist said, bending down and muttering something about leftover DNA in the soil.

But before the scientist could straighten up with his handful of earth, God interrupted him. "Whoa, wait just a minute. You can't use that—get your own dirt."

It is no wonder, really, that Jesus was able to heal the man by the pool in Jerusalem, or calm the storm with a word. These things are no different than a person who makes automobiles simply replacing a flat tire. The wonder is that the sick man existed in the first place, and even the waves upon the sea are a wonder if you come to know enough about them.

A documentary traced the pattern of waves and currents in the oceans of the world. Though they are still mysterious in many ways, it turns out that they are far from random. Cold water melting from the bottom of ice-covered seas near the poles of the earth falls in great unseen vertical rivers straight down to the ocean floor, where it continues to flow through undersea canyons and valleys, and fan out over undersea plains like a giant undetectable flood. This life-giving flow continues nearly all the way around the globe, bringing nutrients and cooling the hot waters at the equator, thus moderating the temperature and weather systems of our planet. Its just one more way the wind and waves obey the One who set them in motion.

I look forward to every little detail the scientists learn. It all makes me marvel even more at the wondrous hand of God at work, and makes me realize anew how utterly we depend on God alone, who made us. Have faith, for we, like the soil from which we came, are in God's loving hands.

Let us pray:
Lord, help us praise you as you deserve, as well as clay pots can praise the potter, for your creative power and awesome love are more than all of science can yet describe, and more than all of the faithful can even yet imagine. Amen.

SUGGESTED PSALM: *Psalm 99*

SUGGESTED HYMNS:

  "I Love to Tell the Story" (B, C, F, L, UM)

  "Let All the World in Every Corner Sing" (B, C, E, P, UM, W)

Mission Accomplished

Hearing the Word

The common theme for today is the choice between rejecting and accepting Christ, and through Christ, God's message. Of course, Jesus encountered various reactions to his teachings, just as any public speaker would. The lesson scripture for today (from Mark 6:1-13) tells about Jesus teaching in his hometown synagogue and being rejected by the people there. As a result of their lack of belief, his power to work miracles there was limited. In the devotional scripture from John's Gospel (12:44-50), Jesus is telling his disciples that those who don't receive him are also rejecting the Father, who sent him, but those who receive Jesus are also receiving the Father.

Living the Word

A kindergarten teacher told her students to make a drawing of something or someone who was important to them. The teacher then walked around the room looking at the students' papers, engaging them in conversation to learn about the things and people who were important to them.

One little girl was deeply involved in the project, coloring fervently, but the teacher could not make out the subject of her artwork. So she asked, and the girl replied, "I'm drawing God."

"But," the teacher protested, "nobody knows what God looks like."

Without looking up from her work, the girl replied, "They will in a minute."

Jesus said, "Whoever sees me sees also him who sent me" (John 12:45). How will people know what God looks like? Or more to the point, how will people know what God is like? We can see God's nature through Jesus. Jesus came as the Word of God made flesh. That way we can come to know God, since God became one of us.

It reminds me of the foreign exchange program for high school youth. In our community, we once hosted a student from Africa. Even though his English sounded strange to us and he was the only person of color in our town, he was active in many school events, and soon got to know many people. He quickly made friends, and suddenly his continent was more than just a distant and unknown land. It had a face and a name, and was forever linked in our minds with our friend. Knowing him, we got to know more about Africa. It was no longer an idea of a distant place, but it became a person for us represented in this youth.

Christianity is an idea for many people. Perhaps they think it is a noble idea that all church-going people fail to live up to, and are therefore hypocrits. Perhaps they think it is a wonderful idea, a way to promote good morals and civility in the world between would-be enemies. Perhaps they think it is nothing to take seriously. Whatever anybody else thinks, it will be either confirmed or challenged by the record of your life! Our witness in the world is either a confirmation of the reality of our faith, or a denial of the validity of it. If our lives show that our beliefs have no impact, and make no difference, then it is testimony of the most powerful kind that states it is wrong, or at best optional.

On the other hand, if our lives are a witness to the importance of our faith, if people can see God's love at work in our daily faith walk, and if it is easy to see that our values are shaped by our desires to live in accordance with God, then God and his kingdom are made visible through us.

It is awesome to think that just as Jesus came to make God known to the world, one important purpose of our life is to make God's love visible and tangible in the world today. Let's pray that when people observe us, from how we handle ourselves around the children to the way we spend our money, they will say, "When I see my friend's life, I can see God at work."

Let us pray:
Lord, may people who know us see you at work in our life. Save us from living a life that is a rebuttal to your love and grace. Instead, help us to reinforce your message through all of our actions. In Christ, amen.

SUGGESTED PSALM: *Psalm 37:1-4, 25-31*
SUGGESTED HYMNS:
  "O Jesus, I Have Promised" (B, C, E, F, L, P, UM)
  "Come Down, O Love Divine" (E, L, P, UM, W)

Impurity Comes from Within

Hearing the Word

Psalm 51 is a psalm of repentance. It speaks of the importance of an inward change of attitudes and values (it is contrasted to the outward repentance of sacrificing animals for the forgiveness of sins). Since such sacrifice was common in Israel, and this seems almost critical of cultic rites (see verse 16), it may be that there were different groups within the faith who placed more of an emphasis on one or the other (inward change or keeping outward rituals). It is certainly in keeping with the lesson scripture for today from Mark. In that case, Jesus is in conflict with the Pharisees. Like Psalm 51, Jesus is critical of trusting in external ceremonies when the most important elements of our faith are inward, spiritual changes.

Living the Word

One of the most fascinating stories of 2001 somehow escaped the limelight. It made *Newsweek* magazine on March 19, 2001, but grabbed less than half of page 35.

It was called "Inside the Spy Tunnel," bringing to light one of the secret missions of the Cold War between the Soviet Union and the United States. Outwardly, we let the Soviet Union construct an embassy complex in Washington, D.C. It was a large white building with neat windows and impeccable landscaping. People passing by in cars outside the grounds might have thought it looked like a peaceful place, and a peaceful gesture between countries who were struggling for a sense of military security in the midst of a blossoming and threatening nuclear arsenal.

But underground, there was no sense of peace. In secret, our government spent over 250 million of our tax dollars to dig a tunnel under the building. The tunnel was not easy to dig, either. It had to be dug silently, so nobody in the building above would figure out that we were "invading" the land we had given them. Like a burglar sneaking into a house at night while trying not to wake up the sleeping family, we were invading from underground.

The reason this project was undertaken was so that, using sophisticated listening devices from underground, we could hear them type on their encoding machine, and help decode their messages back and forth to Russia. But the real reason was that our relationship above ground was different from our relationship below ground. Above ground we were seeking to reach agreements for treaties to slow or stop the insane pace at which both sides were bankrupting themselves to produce weapons of mass destruction. In short, above ground we were seeking to win each other's trust and cooperation, as we should have been. We were working to create a good, or at least better, relationship, for the good of our planet and so our grandchildren did not have to grow up wearing antiradiation outfits.

But underground we did not trust them at all, and we were not acting in a trustworthy way either. I don't know about you, but I think I would have trouble believing they really were my friend after that tunnel thing.

The spy tunnel, it seems to me, illustrates the scripture perfectly. Don't be a Christian in appearance only. Don't come to the door, all smiles and pretending to be God's friend, when inside you are filled with distrust and enmity. You might be able to deceive the people at the Russian embassy, but there is no deceiving God. God doesn't just look at our outward appearance, to see how well we clean up on Sunday mornings for church. God looks at the heart, and God is looking for someone who wants to grow closer to God in love and faithfulness.

Let us pray:
Lord, save us from thinking we could ever hide anything from you, from our bitter feelings to our outward deeds. Instead, help us trust in your forgiving love, and draw near to you in faith. Through Christ, amen.

READ IN YOUR BIBLE: *Luke 19:28-40*   **April 6, 2003**

SUGGESTED PSALM: *Psalm 118:19-29*

SUGGESTED HYMNS:

"*Praise to the Lord, the Almighty*" (B, E, F, L, P, UM,W)

"*O Master, Let Me Walk with Thee*" (B, C, E, F, L, P, UM)

Purifying the Worshiping Community

Hearing the Word

The lesson and devotion scriptures today center on the story of Jesus' triumphant entry into Jerusalem, which we know as Palm Sunday. The chant of the people was based on Psalm 118, and yet the crowd apparently misunderstood the intentions of Jesus as he entered Jerusalem. They were looking for someone to lead them as a great warrior to overcome the Romans, their political oppressors. In fact, years later the people did revolt against the mighty Roman Empire with predictable and bad consequences. In any case, Jesus won a far greater victory for them and for all of humankind. In the midst of the joyous parade of praise for Christ, there is already a hint of the conflict to come as the Pharisees are already in the crowd, criticizing him for letting his disciples make a scene.

Living the Word

Palm Sunday is the most inconsistent day on the Christian calendar. Which do you shout, "Halleluia" or "Watch out!"?

On one hand, it is a joyful parade; many churches have children walk in, waving palm branches and singing happy songs of praise. On the other hand, Jesus knew he was walking a road that would lead to his death.

It is the only Sunday where pastors who follow the lectionary readings (scripture readings that are suggested for a particular Sunday) get two entirely different sets of readings. One set deals with the joyous celebration of Jesus coming into Jerusalem, but the other deals with his betrayal, trial, and death by crucifixion! So pastors get to choose which will be the theme for the day: Do you want to focus on the parade or the sacrifice; do you want to celebrate, or worry?

Have you ever gone to a parade, but had to keep one eye on the darkening skies? You had fun watching the children wave at the people in the parade and scramble for candy, but on the other hand, the gusts of wind and the thunder of the approaching storm kept making you glance up at the sky and wondering if you should grab the kids and make a run for the car. To me, that captures the feelings of Palm Sunday, and in a way, of many circumstances in life.

Sometimes people have to look forward to surgery, or to finding out the results of a worrisome medical test. Sometimes children and youth have to worry about upcoming final exams, or a major project, or getting over their girlfriend or boyfriend deciding to break up with them. Money worries or marriage problems can certainly put a cloud over everything else. And at times most people even worry about death—either their own or a loved one's. These are all clouds that threaten to rain on our parade.

It is probably not healthy to ignore either aspect of Palm Sunday—either the parade or the clouds. If we pretend there are no worries and challenges in life, then we are in denial and fail to deal with them. Besides, they at least make us appreciate the good times. On the other hand, if we dwell only on the storms, we will never have any joy or fun!

I think it is inspiring that Jesus, even knowing he was walking a road that would lead to his death, still celebrated life. He didn't come into town pouting or with furrowed brow. He came with a smile and brought joy to others! So don't spend all your time and energy worrying about either death or taxes—it is better if we too can approach life with a smile and bring joy to others! Take time to sing the happy birthday song to someone, or ride a horse, or just sit on the porch for a while with someone you love and savor the parade of life as it goes down the street.

Let us pray:
Lord, thank you for showing us how to celebrate life, even in the midst of trouble. Please be with those who have worries and burdens that hang over them today like clouds. Help us sing your praises too, not only with our mouth, but also with our daily lives. Amen.

   "Let Us Break Bread Together" (B, E, F, L, P, UM, W)
   "Blest Be the Tie That Binds" (B, C, F, L, P, UM)

New Meaning for Old Traditions

Hearing the Word

The story of Jesus eating the Passover meal with his disciples is one of the events that is unusual because it is found in all four Gospels. Today's devotional text includes the disciples' preparation of the place and the meal, and then the famous Last Supper itself. Today's lesson scripture tells of the same event; parallels can also be found in Luke 22:7-23 and John 13:21-30. One important difference is that John's Gospel features washing the disciples' feet instead of commemorating the bread and wine at the Last Supper, and John then includes a very lengthy last speech from Jesus that is missing in Matthew, Mark, and Luke. Another account of the Last Supper, which stresses the bread and wine, can be found in 1 Corinthians 11:23-25. These scriptures form the basis for the celebration of Holy Communion today.

Living the Word

Some so-called forgiveness is like a dry chalkboard eraser. You wipe away the writing on the chalkboard, but you can still see it dimly showing through the new writing. But genuine forgiveness is like washing the chalkboard at the end of the day with wet cloths. After it dries, you cannot read anything that was written on it during that whole day. It is like a brand new chalkboard.

All grudges will eventually be forgotten; there are no exceptions. It's true! You may be thinking of someone you know who has been able to remember a grudge for a long time, and many people have that talent. But a grudge can only be maintained as

69

long as a person lives. That is why it will eventually be forgotten. Either we forget it while we are alive, or we take it with us to the grave, and there it will be forgotten. After all, even if someone carved all the grudges they were carrying with them on their tombstone, who would care? Remember, a grudge cannot last forever, so why not forget it while it helps you, and your relationships, to do so?

Forgiveness is just the opposite; it is not genuine unless it lasts forever. To really let another person off the hook, so that their mistake no longer continues to poison your relationship with them, would mean that it was left in the past, and the relationship was restored, not in part, but completely. That means no barbed jokes years later, no under-the-belt verbal jabs, no reminders. It would mean that when the thought returns to us, we regard it as an enemy to an ideal relationship with that person, and we deliberately put it out of our mind. We refuse to let the memory of the past invade the present, and wound us all over again.

I know that sounds like dreaming. It is possible, and yet for most of us, there are some situations in which such forgiveness is beyond our grasp. The only way we could achieve it is to ask God for help. After all, if anyone could help us forgive completely, it must be God.

It is amazing that God is able to offer that kind of forgiveness to us! When we seek to renew a good relationship with God through forgiveness and communion, God really leaves our sins in the past, never to be held against us again.

Jesus ate with sinners. He extended forgiveness to known sinners. He dipped his bread at the Last Supper with the man who would betray him, and he still loved Peter even though he knew that Peter, his future church leader, would three times fearfully deny that he knew Jesus. He even prayed for those who crucified them, and asked God not to hold their sins against them.

When God forgives, it lasts forever. Let us try to put that kind of forgiveness into practice with someone we know, someone who really could use the chance to be let off the hook in our mind, not temporarily, but forever.

Let us pray:
Lord, forgive us our sins, as we forgive those who sin against us. Amen.

SUGGESTED PSALM: *Psalm 100*

SUGGESTED HYMNS:

"*Christ the Lord Is Risen Today*" *(All)*

"*Jesus Christ Is Risen Today*" *(E, F, L, P, W)*

Triumph Over Adversity

Hearing the Word

Today being Easter Sunday, there is little doubt about what the devotional and lesson scriptures will focus on! The devotional text, from John 20, records Jesus' appearance to Mary in the garden. Even though it has some parallels in the other Gospels (the Resurrection story in Mark is today's lesson scripture), it goes into more detail about Mary's experience at the tomb than any of the other Gospel writers. There are intriguing discrepancies, as you might expect from an event that is traumatic in many ways and also experienced by several different people. For example, why could Mary not grab on to Jesus in John's Gospel, but in Matthew the disciples grabbed his feet and worshiped him? Still, the Gospels unite their voices to proclaim that Jesus rose from the dead!

Living the Word

The three "Rs" of education are "reading, 'riting, and 'rithmatic," right? If religion also had three "Rs," then they would have to be "resurrection," "recognition," and "response." Resurrection is God's part. It is the first of the three-part miracle of Easter. It is the part that comes to mind when most people think of Easter. The first miracle is that God raised Jesus from the dead! It's what makes the day a special occasion, certainly worth celebrating!

But there is a second part to the Easter miracle. This part has to happen within us. Notice in the Resurrection stories how many of the disciples did not recognize Jesus at first. That has always seemed strange to me! How could they not see him when they were standing right next to him in a locked room, or when he was cooking breakfast for them on the beach, or walking with them on the road to Emmaus, or in Mary's case, standing in the cemetery like the gardener might? Evidently he did not look like they expected him to look. Just think what their lives would have been like if they had failed to recognize him? Suppose Mary just went on thinking Jesus was the gardener! How would the rest of her life have turned out? Suppose the disciples on the road just let Jesus keep on walking once they got to Emmaus, and they had never recognized that God had been walking with them all those miles! Recognition is the second part of the miracle of Easter. If we fail to recognize Jesus, then we miss the power of God's presence walking with us. The opening of our eyes to see the Lord at work, especially in the places we never expected to see God, is a genuine miracle. Recognition is the part that happens when the Lord heals our eyesight, our way of looking at the world, so that we can see him.

The third part of the miracle of Easter is our response. Mary exclaimed "Teacher!" and would have hugged Jesus if she could have. The disciples who had trudged for seven miles by day to Emmaus ran seven miles back to Jerusalem by night to tell others that he had appeared to them! That is quite a response! When Peter realized that it was Jesus on the beach cooking breakfast for him and the other fishermen, the boat couldn't get him there fast enough—he jumped in and swam to shore! All the disciples responded to the Resurrection, to the recognition that the Lord is alive and still at work in the world. They went to work preaching, teaching, healing, and making disciples. They wrote letters of faith and encouraged people and, in a word, started the church! That's quite a response.

Easter is a miracle. Anytime a person who is dead comes back to life, you would have to say that's a miracle worth coming home for. But there is more. May we experience the rest of the miracle, too. May the Lord open our eyes to see him in places we had never expected to see him. And may the Lord help us respond with joy and hope and love, and dedicated service, to the good news that Jesus is alive!

Let us pray:
Lord, on this Easter Sunday, help us celebrate the joy of your resurrection, and see you at work in our world, and join in your mission as we respond with love to what you have done for us! In the name of the risen Christ. Amen.

READ IN YOUR BIBLE: *Hebrews 11:1-6*   **April 27, 2003**

SUGGESTED PSALM: *Psalm 33:1-9*

SUGGESTED HYMNS:

"Onward Christian Soldiers" (B, C, E, F, L, UM)

"Jesus Shall Reign" (All)

Faith Conquers Fear

Hearing the Word

The book of Hebrews could have been written by the apostle Paul or by someone else—most scholars lean toward it being someone else. The book is placed in the New Testament order directly between Paul's known writings and the writings that are authored by other writers. Whoever wrote it addressed the letter to the "Hebrews," in general—it is apparently not intended for any particular church or individual. In this section, the writer assumes a working understanding of the Jewish scriptures (our Old Testament) as they interpret the meaning of faith. Faith could be understood in this minisermon as believing something that is not seen (and today we might add something not provable scientifically), or it could be understood as a trusting relationship between us and God.

Living the Word

The quotation "April showers bring May flowers" came up in a conversation I had with a farmer. He mentioned the saying near the end of our conversation. I guess he was trying to be optimistic, trying to be lighthearted. But on that day, the April showers were a harsh reality.

To put it bluntly, he was frustrated, and I don't blame him. After a few relatively dry, warm days, that particular day was going to be the first he could get into his fields, he said. He told me all about the work he had been intending to do. But instead we were standing inside having this conversation, and outside the rain just kept coming.

April showers happen to everyone. You know it when you feel

like complaining, when you feel flooded and overwhelmed by adversity, when factors beyond your control have a negative impact on you. The saying is for the days when all you can see is unwelcome rain, and the flowers you picture are just a dream, a hope. The saying affirms that good things can grow out of rough times—the rain in April may be unpleasant at times, but it does pave the way for flowers in May.

A parishioner went through the line one Sunday and complimented me on the sermon. "I don't know how you do it," she added, referring to part of the sermon that personally meant something to her. The truth is that preparing a weekly sermon often proves the old saying, "Creativity is 10 percent inspiration and 90 percent perspiration!" It is amazing how God can step in and use those April showers of Saturday night nerves and still make use of the worst sermon you've ever written to lift somebody's spirit.

Other occupations have their April showers too. Teachers get appreciated now and then by parents and students, and I'm sure they take pride in seeing their students use their education to better their lives. But have you ever tried facing twenty-five noisy grade-school kids for hours when you had a splitting headache? Have you ever needed to stay up late at night grading papers and preparing to teach, even after some parent griped at you because their child didn't get the grade they expected? Teachers have their April showers, but through it all, their work and even their headaches pave the way for the May flowers of graduation.

"April showers bring May flowers" is not a saying found in the Bible. But it reflects a Christian belief we might express in this Easter season. There are many aspects of life that are really hard. Some seem impossible. Others are frustrating or depressing. Many are out of our control, like rain for days on end. But so often, God is able to take our adverse circumstances and make something good happen through them. We just have to see through the rain, which is obvious, to the dream of the flowers, which we can only see with the eyes of faith.

Let us pray:
Lord, in this Easter season, help us bring to you all of the stress, worry, fear, and grief in our life, all of which we can see all too well. Help us trust you to transform every problem into something still unseen, but something that we know will be an even greater joy. Amen.

"I Sing the Almighty Power of God" (B, E, P, UM, W)
"O God, Our Help in Ages Past" (All)

Act Boldly in Faith

Hearing the Word

The story of Jesus healing the Roman officer's servant is more than a story about a miraculous healing made even more incredible because it was performed from a long distance. It is the story of the faith that an outsider to the Jewish faith had. Jesus makes a point that this man's faith is even greater than any he has seen in Israel. Likewise, the story in today's lesson scripture (Mark 7:24-37) is the story of an outsider's faith. In this case, it was a Gentile woman who sought Jesus' help for her daughter. In her case, Jesus seemed to resist helping her, but she persisted in such a way that Jesus was evidently persuaded by her hope and faith to help her, and he did.

Living the Word

A couple of catfish *(Albino Coryadoras)* laid eggs in my son's aquarium. Sometimes she selects a wide-leafed plant or a rock, leaving the adhesive eggs stuck to the surface much like putting a sticky note on a refrigerator. I was amused that she decided to stick one batch on the shell of the big snail. The irony is that those were the only eggs I could rescue from the tank. The rest were promptly eaten by other fish. The world can be a mighty tough place for little ones. That's true not only for catfish, but also for people.

Consider these statistics: In our world today, malnutrition kills an estimated thirty-two thousand children every day, year-round. During the last decade, wars have killed about two million children, disabled between four and five million children, made more than five million children into refugees, and made more than twelve million homeless. More children than soldiers now die from war.

These statistics do not tell the most common stories, either. Some children simply feel lonely, or sad, or rejected by their peers. Some battle against physical or mental limitations. The list of challenges that today's children must face is incredibly long.

I write this because probably none of these children are yours. But just as Jesus reached out beyond his circle of responsibility to help the Roman officer's servant and the Gentile woman's daughter (in the lesson scripture), it is good for followers of Jesus to care for others beyond their line of what might be expected.

Do you remember the time in the Bible when Jesus blessed the children? None of those children were his, obviously. The disciples scolded the people who brought their children to Jesus, essentially telling them that Jesus had more important things to do. But Jesus corrected the disciples, letting them know how important the children were to him. Then he blessed them.

Whether you have children or not, you can find ways to have a positive effect in the lives of children, those you happen to know and those who live in hunger or poverty or war-torn areas around the world. It is especially tragic when children, who must depend on adults, suffer when the larger community could have made a difference. The answers can be difficult to find, but don't think that someone else has them! There are more problems out there than you or I can solve, but for some small part of the problem, we are the solution! Our part of the answer may be to volunteer our time to a school or library, or to contribute to an organization that works with children, or just to be a friend and mentor. But in some way, I believe God intends every Christian to be part of the answer.

If a snail can carry a brood of catfish on its back, and be the only hope those little fish had in their watery cruel world, then surely you and I could do something on land where we live. It would be a good thing if today you and I had a talk with the Lord, and started the conversation, "Lord, is there anything you would like me to do, today, in order to make my life a blessing to the little ones in our world?"

Let us pray:
Lord, please use me in any way you can to continue your ministry of loving and blessing the children, both those who live around me and those who live around the world. Amen.

"Be Thou My Vision" (B, E, F, P, UM)
"There's a Wideness in God's Mercy" (All)

Follow in Faith

Hearing the Word

Today's lesson scripture centers on Jesus' question to his disciples, "Who do you say that I am?" The various disciples repeated what others had wondered aloud (such as the great prophet Elijah), but Peter was bold enough to say what he personally thought, and he declared that Jesus was the Messiah, the Son of the Living God. This declaration was a turning point in Peter's life, and in Jesus' ministry too. It took some time for the early disciples and the early church to figure out how to talk about Jesus, and describe him. After all, he was divine, and yet human; even today theologians are still grappling with how to describe the nature of Christ. Meanwhile, the early church put their thoughts in the form of a hymn, which Paul quotes in today's devotional reading in Philippians 2:5-11.

Living the Word

An old joke has the president of the United States visiting a city on a public relations outing. The president is bored, however, and says to his driver, "James, you have been driving me around for years now, and I never get to drive. Get in the backseat and let me drive this big limo for awhile!"

The driver gave in and got in the backseat. The president hit the gas and went over sixty miles an hour through a school zone.

Sure enough, at the edge of town a sheriff's deputy noticed the black limo speeding through the school zone, and pulled it over. When he asked for a driver's license, he suddenly realized what he had done. "Just a minute, sir," he stammered. Then he went back to his car and radioed the sheriff. "Sir," he began, "I've made a terrible mistake and pulled over someone who is very important. And I mean important!"

The sheriff asked, "Who? The mayor?"

"No."

"Well, then who do you think it is?"

"I don't know, sir, but the president of the United States is his driver!"

A pivotal moment in Jesus' ministry came when, at Caesarea Phillipi, he asked his disciples, "Who do people say that I am?" After they repeated all the gossip on the subject from down at the corner diner, Jesus went on to ask them, "Who do you say that I am?" This made the question personal. Instead of taking a poll or survey, Jesus was interested in knowing where he stood with the disciples.

Throughout the centuries, the church has institutionalized the answer to that question. We have various creeds that affirm what we believe. The first two (of three) parts of the Apostle's Creed: "I believe in God the Father Almighty, maker of heaven and earth; and in Jesus Christ his only Son our Lord; who was conceived by the Holy Spirit, born of the Virgin Mary, suffered under Pontius Pilate, was crucified, dead, and buried; he ascended into heaven, and sitteth at the right hand of God the Father Almighty; from thence he shall come to judge the quick and the dead."

In the devotional text for today Paul quotes what is apparently an early hymn of the church that expresses the official position of the church about who Jesus is. However, even reciting an official church position is not what makes us Christians. The key is our answer to the question from Christ, "Who do you say that I am?" In some way, we answer this question every day. By our words, our actions, our scheduling, our priorities, and even our checkbooks, we answer this question. Either Jesus is our Lord, or he is something lesser to us.

Let us pray:

Lord, help us have a personal faith like Peter's, so that we may know without a doubt who you are to us, and how important you are to our life. Help us proclaim your lordship over our life by all we say and do each day, so that nobody has to ask us who you are to us. This we pray through Christ our Lord. Amen.

Facing Our Unbelief

Hearing the Word

It is difficult to picture the exact setting for this speech, except it is obvious that it is given near the end of Jesus' life. He has spoken for most of his ministry in parables and sayings, but now he is attempting to speak plainly to his disciples so they will understand, even though they still don't quite seem to. It is striking that after listening to Jesus for as long as three years, they still do not understand what is to come, even when Jesus attempts to explain it to them plainly. They sort of understand, just like the man in the lesson scripture who replies honestly to the question whether he believes by stating, "I believe, Lord, but help my unbelief."

Living the Word

In May, 2000, the Scripps Howard News Service carried a story about a woman who believed that a miracle had occurred in her front yard. It started one day while some people had gathered and were drinking in the front yard. One man suddenly got up and stared at a knot in an olive tree, cleaned his glasses, looked at it again. He finally decided he had better go home because he must have had too much to drink. He thought he was seeing an image of the Virgin Mary in a darkened shape in the center of the knot.

Others looked at it, though, and saw what he meant. To them too it looked like an image of the Virgin Mary. Soon the knot in the tree was a neighborhood attraction. People came to leave flowers and candles, and to pray in front of the tree.

Soon some of the people began to ask their church officials what they thought about it—was it a miracle? The church, through a spokesperson, encouraged people to view the image with "a healthy skepticism." The spokesperson noted that "people are

79

drawn to things that they feel bring them closer to God. The only danger would be in putting your faith or your trust or your hope in what may be caused by natural means and may not be a spiritual phenomenon."

A close-up photo of the knot in the tree does reveal a vertical darkened area in the center of the knot. However, to the skeptical eye, it is hard to tell, at least from the photo, whether she is holding an umbrella and ducking to avoid the rain, or standing tall and cradling a baby in her arms, or waving with her right arm, or kneeling to look in the manger. Then again, photographers don't interpret reality for you. They just take an objective picture of it; what you see in it is up to you.

One of the things I see in the story, as one who understands the official church's skeptical response, is that once there were people sitting around drinking in the front yard, and now they feel closer to God and are taking time to pray to God. That in itself does not prove God's existence or disprove it, just as the stain in the knothole does not finally decide the outcome of whether God is alive and well on planet earth.

Jesus wanted his followers to see all of life in a new way. Sometimes they were so slow to understand that they could not have recognized a miracle if one came up and bonked them on the head. It is actually refreshing to think that they were often so slow to understand, and yet Jesus still turned over the Kingdom to these disciples. Maybe they missed a miracle now and then, or couldn't figure out what it meant, but on the other hand, he saw in them people who were changing, who wanted to walk with him.

I don't think the worst mistake is to read a miracle into something that might not be one. I think it is to be surrounded by the miraculous and still not believe. Even a knothole, with or without a dark stain, if you think about it, is a miracle. It is the place where a branch died, but God healed the tree. As the man in the front yard did, let us clean our glasses, and take another close look, with the eyes of faith, at the world around us.

Let us pray:
Lord, open my eyes today to see your wondrous hand at work in so many ways all around us, that we may not pass by the miraculous and think it is nothing special. We believe, but help us in our unbelief too. Amen.

READ IN YOUR BIBLE: *John 20:24-31*   **May 25, 2003**

SUGGESTED PSALM: *Psalm 126*

SUGGESTED HYMNS:

"Christ the Lord Is Risen Today" (All)

"The Strife Is O'er, the Battle Done" (B, E, L, P, UM, W)

How Bold Is Your Faith?

Hearing the Word

Through the breathtaking series of resurrection appearances, Jesus has appeared first to Mary Magdalene, then Peter and John (the writer of the Gospel), then the rest of the disciples except Thomas (who doubted what the others said when they told him), and then to Thomas too, helping him believe. Finally, John makes his appeal directly to the reader to have faith. He explains that he has written everything down with the reader in mind, which is usually the point of writing, hoping that the reader would have faith. The lesson scripture tells the story of how Jesus healed the blind man. Jesus told him his faith made him well. Both biblical texts share the theme of seeing is believing, and the importance of believing even before we see Jesus face-to-face.

Living the Word

Seeing is believing. If doubting Thomas didn't coin the phrase, he should have. It is perfect for him, and for many of us too.

This is one approach to life. You lose your job at 9:00 A.M., and at lunch you tell your friend all about it. Suddenly your friend promises that he will talk to his boss, because he thinks his boss ought to hire another person. For some people, the natural answer is, "I'll believe it when I see it." Is that a poor attitude? Maybe, but it is understandable.

Agent to artist: "This will be a great deal. It is a great company, and they are capable of making you a lot of money." Artist: "I'll believe it when I cash the check." In the freelance world, you learn not to spend your money before you have it.

And who could blame Thomas for his answer? "Jesus is risen!" his friends told him. But really, how often do dead people escape the grave? "I'll believe it when I see it," he replied. That's one approach to life, the safe, defensive, and don't-let-yourself-be-disappointed approach. It is living in a world where you expect death and disappointment, so it doesn't surprise you or hurt you quite as much when your worst expectations come to pass.

There is also another approach, which the disciples modeled as time went by. I think it took the Resurrection to jar them into it, but it is called seeing what you believe. This is a visionary way of looking at life. It is just as aware of the disappointment and death out there, but it chooses to picture something different. If you try to see the world as you believe it should be, you might get disappointed and maybe hurt. But you will be picturing, participating in, and working for, new life.

The unemployed man will see, instead of the probable disappointment of a job that has not even been created yet, the chance to be first in line for a new position, and to help write the job description to fit his strengths. He will see the life of a friend who is genuinely trying to help him, and who will stand by him with or without this opportunity working out. He will see that it only takes one opportunity to work out to become employed again, and meanwhile, he will see that he can seek other opportunities in case this one does not work.

The artist can feel sorry that deals are unlikely to be as successful as the agent always makes them sound, or get to work to broaden the opportunity into something better and bigger than the agent or the client ever thought about.

Nobody can really blame Thomas for doubting. Anyone can assemble a long string of life experiences that give evidence for those who expect the worst, and choose to see nothing else.

To change that kind of thinking, it would almost take a person rising from the dead, and telling us that God is on our side, and that there is no problem or difficulty that will be able to outlast God's ability to turn it into a triumph. Look out into the world, and practice seeing what you believe!

Let us pray:
Lord, in this Easter season, lift our eyes with hope, and lift our spirits with your presence, that we may believe. With you, may we continue fulfilling your vision of abundant life for the entire world. In the name of our risen Lord, Jesus Christ, we pray and seek this. Amen.

SUGGESTED PSALM: *Psalm 145*

SUGGESTED HYMNS:

"*Stand Up, Stand Up for Jesus*" *(B, C, E, F, L, UM)*
"*Amazing Grace*" *(All)*

Facing a God-given Opportunity

Hearing the Word

This vision was written to comfort the people who were in exile in Babylonia, and reading between the lines, to motivate them to leave, too. Being conquered and taken as prisoners was a humiliating defeat, and crushing to the ongoing practice of their faith. On the other hand, as time went by, they got used to living in their new land. As some of the Israelites in the desert had wished they were back in slavery in Egypt, so some of the exiles might have chosen living in exile over interrupting their known life and starting a new one. The effect of hearing these beautiful words would make them remember the joy and the hope involved in returning to the promised land, and thereby motivate them to leave their current homes.

Living the Word

One time the clergy of my whole area were required to attend a meeting that was scheduled to last for three days. It was the idea of the hierarchy to get all the clergy to converge on Decatur, Illinois, and have six hundred pastors volunteer to do a bunch of work with the poor in that town as a way to make a witness to the community. To be honest, I didn't want to go. I whined and griped a little. In talking to some of my clergy friends, I discovered that they were complaining too! After all, it was three full days smack dab in the middle of a busy week.

But we all went. The first thing I ran into was six hundred clergy standing in line to register. It seems great minds think alike. If registration is from 10:30 until noon, why not come at 11:55?

About an hour later, with our stomachs growling, we had communion together. The speaker compared the mandatory attendance to a mother making her children turn off the TV and come to dinner. She said that she knew many of us felt too busy to come, but that it was still good for our relationships with each other and with God to come as a family to the table.

That evening, someone from the city government told us that in that first day, we had given more than 2,400 hours of service to schools, churches, and agencies that work with the poor in Decatur. That amounted to sixty full-time, 40-hour weeks of volunteer service. I was assigned to a first-grade classroom at a church-related school. I helped bury a fish that jumped out of the tank, and got to tell them the story of Moses, and help them with their reading skills. One little boy grabbed my hand the minute I walked in the door. He hugged me once, and his teacher reminded him that he was allowed only two hugs a day. Later, she explained that he had been abused by his natural parents. Now living with foster parents, he craves positive adult attention. He's limited to two hugs a day because, she said, otherwise he would cling to her all day. Suddenly the long drive seemed a lot more worthwhile!

There were many other meaningful things that happened, and I came home feeling inspired and blessed. I got to know some of the children in the poor parts of Decatur in person. I played with them and told them a story. It reminded me of the real struggles some kids face just to feel loved by the squeeze of a adult's hand. Like a kid compelled to turn off the TV and come to dinner, I complained. Then God blessed me anyway!

Like the Israelites who resisted leaving their homes in exile in Babylonia to come resettle the promised land, we often drag our feet when it comes to the church. It is easy to find excuses to not volunteer, to be too tired to roll out of bed for worship, or to be too busy to serve on a committee. Those are exactly the times when it is important to give God the chance to bless you.

Let us pray:
Lord, forgive us for dragging our feet and complaining so much about change, about trying something new or different. For we know you have called us with a happy heart, and simply want to lead us to greener pastures where we will surely be blessed by you. Amen.

READ IN YOUR BIBLE: *Psalm 100:1-5*   **June 8, 2003**
SUGGESTED PSALM: *Psalm 138*
SUGGESTED HYMNS:
 "All Hail the Power of Jesus' Name" (All)
 "All Glory, Laud, and Honor" (B, E, F, L, P, UM, W)

Laying Foundations

Hearing the Word

Psalm 100 is a famous and beautiful psalm of thanksgiving. It was written as an *entrance* psalm, one that might be used like we use a call to worship or if it was set to music, a hymn of praise at the beginning of a worship service. Regarding the content, notice that the reason for giving thanks is not a laundry list of blessings, but (and this seems a bit foreign to us these days) because God is the way God is. In other words, God has a character that is praiseworthy. It might be like the events where a bunch of stars get together and pay tribute to a great musician's career. The person is being praised because he or she is a great songwriter or performer, not for having given gifts to the participants. In the same way, God is celebrated for being faithful, good, and loving; a bit different than remembering to say thanks for the food, clothes, shelter, family, church, and other blessings that we enjoy.

Living the Word

Psalm 100 puts into words the goodness of God, and gives us a way to appreciate not only God's deeds, but also God's character. It is a second step of thanks—more than just hurrying out the door after a nice meal and remembering to shout over your shoulder, "Thanks, Mom!" Rather, it is pausing over dinner to look Mom in the eyes, and think about who she is, and how good it is that she has cared for your well-being faithfully all this time, one meal at a time.

I am constantly impressed by the effort that goes into a church meal. There may be thirty people or hundreds of people waiting to be served, but the activity behind the scenes is incredible. Women and men are shuffling rolls into the oven, rinsing off trays, getting baby seats out of the closet, setting out silverware, and breaking up ice. The kitchen crew is usually there by breakfast, and the last one leaves with a load of tablecloths and washcloths to launder, long after the lunch is over.

If all of this is what it takes to give lunch to a hundred or two hundred people, imagine what it would take to feed lunch to the whole world! It would be a task so immense, with arrangements and details so complicated, that literally only God could see that it was done. Simply put, it is the everyday miracle of providing our basic needs. Saying thanks to God is good and appropriate, but we need to go a step further and recognize how great God is for simply having the ability, and the desire, to work this miracle on a daily basis for us.

In short, beyond thanks, there is a relationship of appreciation and admiration that underlies our relationship with God. That is why this is a good psalm to begin worship—before we ever start talking about God's saving acts, we begin by talking about how great God is, and pausing simply to appreciate that fact.

Proverbs 15:17 states that it's, "better to eat vegetables with people you love than to eat the finest meat where there is hate."

This proverb points out that what makes a meal special is the people you are with—not just the food. Whether it be a Thanksgiving feast or fast food with a friend or child, it is good to look up between bites and listen carefully to the other person. It's good to express your love for that person now and then, to say the important positive things you'll always be glad you said instead of using mealtime to criticize.

The most famous meal in the New Testament is the Last Supper Jesus had with his disciples. It was not much of a feast. The menu was only bread and wine. Yet the fellowship at the table was with one whose love is perfect, and so it has become the central meal in the New Testament. Called "the great thanksgiving," it is not merely a thank-you. It is really an opportunity, like we have when we gather around a meal, to fellowship with God, to appreciate who God really is, and to draw nearer to God.

Let us pray:

Lord, thank you for all you do for us, and also, thank you for who you are! We are thankful that you have sought to be with us; it is good to know that you are trustworthy, merciful, and abundant in your love for us. Amen.

READ IN YOUR BIBLE: *1 Corinthians 3:10-17*   **June 15, 2003**
SUGGESTED PSALM: *Psalm 78*
SUGGESTED HYMNS:
  "My Hope Is Built" (B, C, F, L, P, UM)
  "How Firm a Foundation" (All)

Getting Back on Track

Hearing the Word

As a person who began new churches, the apostle Paul compared himself to the workers who lay the foundation for a new building, then turn over the rest of the work to others who come and build upon the foundation. In this analogy, he compared Jesus to the foundation itself, and encouraged others to build upon that solid beginning a structure (or a church community) that would stand the test of time. In a similar way, in today's lesson scripture the prophet Haggai criticized the people of Israel who had moved back to Israel from exile. They were busy building their own homes, but were not exerting much effort to repair the Temple, God's house, which was laying in ruins.

Living the Word

A middle-aged pastor was explaining to his confirmation class why the church took a group picture of them and placed it in the hallway. "This way, when you are old, you can come back to this hallway, and see each other's picture, and remember. You might see Jimmy over there, and think, 'There's Jimmy when he was a kid! Now he's the principal of the high school.' Or maybe you will see Danita's picture when she is this age, and think, 'I remember! That's what Danita looked like back in confirmation class. Now she's running a chain of department stores.'"

One of the youth seemed to understand, and enthusiastically said, "Oh, I get it! And when we're older, we'd see your picture and say, 'Now there's old Rev. Dickerson, our confirmation teacher! Of course, he's dead now.'"

In many churches, especially older ones, we sit in pews we did not buy, meet in buildings we did not build, and benefit from traditions we did not set. There are many people who are dead now, but who in their day built the church, taught the classes, gave sacrificially to keep the church going, helped begin the programs that are old customs now, and so on.

To get a feeling for the history of your church, it is a good idea to sit down with some of the older people, and ask them questions about the church's history, the old customs, and so on. Be sure to have someone take good notes, or better yet, put it on videotape. Of course, their memories can only go back a generation or so. But if you take a walk in the church cemetery, or look back in the old records, just imagine what the names written there could tell you!

In one church I served, the old meeting records were written in old German, so I could not read them. One day I sat down with someone who could read German. She began to read to me about the past of the church. It was exciting to learn about some of the traditions that seem so familiar. And it was equally exciting to hear about the construction of parts of the building that now are old, what the various proposals were, how they made the decisions they did. It was interesting to hear familiar family names of people whose descendants still lived in the community.

She explained what the writing on the old stained-glass window meant, since they too were written in German. The letters were starting to flake away, and someday they will be impossible to read. As time goes by, and our records are lost, fade away, are burned, or misplaced, and our older adults die one at a time.

We owe it to future generations to preserve as much of our history as we can, and to make it available to generations yet to come. It is a precious gift, impossible to recover once it is lost. On the other hand, many layers between ours and the date the foundation was laid are unknown. The one thing we know is that the original foundation of our faith, laid in Paul's day and re-laid in our lives today, is Jesus Christ. He is the foundation, and everything we do in our life and our churches will stand strong if we build on him.

Let us pray:
Lord, remind us that what we build is temporary, unless we build upon your name and holy purpose. Thank you for our history, both known and lost to time, and for all those whose faithful witness has brought us this far. May our lives continue to be a strong witness for you that will stand the test of time. Amen.

READ IN YOUR BIBLE: *Psalm 48:1-14*　　　　　　　**June 22, 2003**

SUGGESTED PSALM: *Psalm 82*

SUGGESTED HYMNS:

　"A Mighty Fortress Is Our God" (All)

　"Open My Eyes, That I May See" (B, C, F, P, UM)

Hope for the Future

Hearing the Word

Many people feel proud of their city, right? This is especially true if their city has a winning professional sports team, or if their city is renowned for anything from "The Big Apple" to "The Hummingbird Capital of the World." The Israelites took pride in the promised land, and especially Jerusalem, and who could blame them? Psalm 48, the devotional scripture, expresses that it was the home city of the Almighty God! In today's lesson scripture, the prophet Zechariah is speaking to the exiles and reassuring them that God will once again return, with them, to the promised land.

Living the Word

One of the more interesting ancient places in North America is Cahokia Mounds near Collinsville, Illinois. The largest prehistoric man-made feature in North America is located there. Called Monk's Mound, it is a dirt pyramid with a huge plateau on top. The plateau is 100 feet high, and at the base, the dirt structure covers fourteen acres! This pile of earth would take quite a while for men in modern earthmoving equipment to create, but the Indians who made it simply carried the dirt in by hand, a sack full at a time! Archaeologists have learned that the plateau held more than one building, made with wood beams sunk into the ground. Apparently the lofty plateau was either a holy temple of some kind, or the home of the chief, or both.

This gigantic mound is not the only one in the area. There are many other earthen mounds that served various purposes over a rich archaeological site that covers miles. Much of the site is still unexcavated, but enough has been uncovered to understand that between A.D. 800 and A.D. 1300, this was a huge city with a population at times of at least twenty thousand. Monk's Mound and the central part of the city was protected during part of that history with a two-mile wall made of nearly twenty thousand vertically placed hickory logs, each about fifteen feet tall and a foot in diameter. Among the mysteries of the site is a huge woodhenge, similar to Stonehenge, apparently used to mark the alignment of the sun at the spring and fall equinoxes.

This civilization was the largest, or one of the largest on earth at the time. Yet somehow it came to an end. Archaeologists don't think they were invaded and taken over. Instead, apparently a gradual change in climate caused problems with growing and gathering enough food. There is evidence of some malnutrition and disease in latter years. Most likely the great city gradually decreased in population until it was finally abandoned. Eventually it was occupied later by other Indians, and before the archaeologists began to study it, the farmer who owned the land actually plowed the land and grew crops on top of the mound!

Since long before the Cahokia Indians built Monk's Mound in North America, Jerusalem has been occupied, destroyed, rebuilt, and reoccupied at various times in its history too. During the periods of time when the Israelites did not live there, they longed for it to be their home. Psalm 48 expresses the pride of the people in the "mountain of God," which was protected by the Almighty God.

Jerusalem has been the religious center for the Jewish people for many centuries, much like Cahokia seemed to be for the Mississippian Indians. However, since Christ, our religious center has changed from an earthly place to a spiritual one. While we honor Jerusalem and the promised land for its rich history and for being the place where Jesus lived, our homeland is now the kingdom of God. Our leader is not lifted up by gloriously living upon a mountain of earth, but by humbling himself through his sacrificial death on the cross.

Let us pray:
Lord, thank you for those earthly places we love and think of as our permanent home. Remind us as we learn about history, that no earthly place is as permanent as trusting in you to provide us a heavenly home, and allowing us to participate in your eternal purposes even now on this earth. Amen.

SUGGESTED PSALM: *Psalm 95*

SUGGESTED HYMNS:

"*O Jesus, I Have Promised*" *(B, C, E, F, L, P, UM)*

"*Come Down, O Love Divine*" *(E, L, P, UM, W)*

Celebrating Victories

Hearing the Word

Psalm 96 is a psalm that would have been used during the enthronement festival. Other nations that had kings would celebrate the enthronement of their king; since Israel's king is God, then it made sense that they would enthrone God over their nation and life through a worship service. This psalm is particularly appropriate to go along with the lesson scripture today (Ezra 5–6), which is the celebration of the completion of the new Temple in Jerusalem following the Exile (in keeping with the progression of readings in recent weeks).

Living the Word

For those who may be unfamiliar with the structure of The United Methodist Church, you might be interested to know why our highest church officials lose their voice and their vote when they take the office of "bishop." The decision was heavily influenced by the ideas of those who were working on our American form of government at the time.

Methodism was born in England when John Wesley and some other students at Oxford began a holiness club to encourage one another to read their Bibles, pray, and practice other spiritual disciplines more regularly. They were studying to become ministers in the Church of England, which had a hierarchical structure. And of course the government of England had kings and queens.

As the holiness clubs multiplied and eventually spread overseas to the colonists, John Wesley tried to retain direct control over his growing movement. Even though he could not directly supervise every group, he wanted to have a say in how the leaders ran their groups.

When the Methodists in America adopted the constitution of their new church, they incorporated many of the ideas of the American Constitution, including the balance of powers between the three branches of government. Bishops are as high of an office as any clergy can attain, but to stay away from anything that seemed at all like a king, those who become bishops are not allowed to vote on any legislative matters. Further, they are not allowed to speak either for or against any pending legislation when it is being debated. And there are numerous bishops—when you put them all together, they form the Council of Bishops, so no one particular bishop has any rank or authority over the other bishops. The church therefore has no one official spokesperson—it can officially speak only by committees or groups.

All this is not to say that it is a better or worse structure than other denominations have, but it is interesting how the effects of the war with England, and America's rejection of English rule, rubbed off on the structure of the American church.

Having a king can be good, or it can be bad. If the king has great ideas and is given the unilateral power of carrying them out, then a kingdom can flourish under leadership that is not hindered by things like gridlock between feuding political parties. On the other hand, if a king is not so good, then that is a lot of power to give someone who is incompetent, or worse, malevolent. America decided it wasn't worth the risk.

When we allow God to be our "king," however, we are giving our loyalty to, and agreeing to be subject to one who loves us. God is obviously an effective leader, able to guide us in good directions and strong enough to carry out God's purposes.

The Israelites enthroned God in their festival. To us, as we read this psalm, we can think of God as the perfect king, one who is powerful enough to govern with justice and mercy, kind enough to fill our lives with good things, and one who deserves our love and loyalty.

Let us pray:
Lord, forgive us for kneeling before the throne of money or power or any other idolatrous image that we may call good and let rule our life. Instead help us acknowledge you and follow your ways, that we may place our confidence and faith and loyalty in you alone. Amen.

SUGGESTED PSALM: *Psalm 127:1-2*
SUGGESTED HYMNS:
  "Lord, I Want to Be a Christian" (B, C, F, P, UM)
  "Holy God, We Praise Thy Name" (E, F, L, P, UM, W)

Accepting a Challenging Task

Hearing the Word

In ancient times, the walls around a city inspired feelings of security. They were the difference between being ransacked and having an abundant life in safety. Isaiah weaves this prophecy, in part, around the image of the city walls. They stand strong and protect the righteous, but those who are proud (those who look to themselves instead of to God for their security and meaning) will have their walls torn down. Those who the proud oppressed will trample the walls underfoot, while those who honor the Lord will have a smooth path in life. All of this comes from the realization that God is going to see that justice is finally done, and all of this comes from the conviction that real security is to be found in God alone. The lesson scripture for today is about the decision to rebuild the walls around Jerusalem by Nehemiah, which fits together with the devotional scripture in Isaiah.

Living the Word

There was a double murder not far from where we live. Many people here in this rural area said that after they heard about the murders, and particularly during the time the police were still looking for these men, they decided to lock the doors of their homes. We did too, but that's really just a false sense of security, isn't it? If desperate murderers wanted to get into a house, a door lock wouldn't stop them.

One of the things that made this crime so shocking is that so many of us think of our little town as a safe place. In fact, prior to the murders, residents didn't bother to lock their doors, and some people even left their keys in their car ignition round the clock! So this violent crime had the effect of knocking down the imaginary walls of security we have built in our minds around our town. They were comforting, but now they have been violated, and this violation makes us question whether they can be relied upon.

Real security is probably not possible on this earth, especially if we are talking about security from physical or mental harm. Where is our security to be found? Can God build a wall around us that will keep us safe from all of the perils of the world?

God is not in the business of providing protection from everything that might be bad, because that would mean we would have to live in a world where nothing evil or sinful ever occurred. That would mean we could not live in this world where we have been given free choice to love God or reject God.

On the other hand, we can have security, not in walls or locks, but through our relationship with God. In God's kingdom, we will eventually not have to live in fear of anything, and we won't seek to find our security in walls or locks. No security guards will be needed to keep the have-nots from trying to take by force the bounty of the haves of the world. No murderers or robbers will commit senseless crimes. No nations will be at war with one another, no children will be killed in border disputes. No racial or economic walls will create suspicion and hostility and pain, because we will all trust the Lord together, and know what it means to truly love our brothers and sisters.

To be wise, lock your doors, and be alert, and be careful. The perfectly safe kingdom of God is not here yet—not even in small quiet towns. Don't look for security in the wrong places. It can be found in God alone, by doing God's will, by seeking justice instead of protection, by seeking love instead of hostility, and in the full implementation of the kingdom of God.

Let us pray:

Lord, forgive us for building walls to separate ourselves from others, whether those walls are built of brick or hatred or fear. Forgive us for seeking security through separation and enforcement of an unfair distribution of goods. Instead, let us seek peace with justice, safety through reconciliation with others, and the security of living in a community that is determined to do your will. Amen.

   "Blessed Assurance" (B, C, F, P, UM)
   "My Faith Looks Up to Thee" (B, C, E, F, L, P, UM)

Persevering with Faith

Hearing the Word

In Isaiah, chapters 40 and beyond are addressed to the Israelite people while they are in exile. Isaiah's theme is to give the people hope that their relationship with God will continue and they will one day be restored to their land. Isaiah's moving words in this section are among the most beautiful expressions in the Bible of God's love in the midst of tragedy. He refers to the rebuilding and restoration of Israel, which fits in with the lesson scripture for today, Nehemiah 6. In that section of Nehemiah, the people are successfully rebuilding the wall around Jerusalem in spite of opposition from Israel's enemies.

Living the Word

My grandmother died this year after a long and good life. She was my last grandparent, so it meant saying good-bye to a generation. She lived in the same house all of her life, about 90 years, so as her house and all her possessions are sorted and distributed among the family or auctioned off, it is also saying good-bye to an important part of what all of us have always called home.

All of her life, she attended a little stone church at the end of her block. It was right past the cemetery, so you had to walk past all those people who had died before going to hear the word of life. Late in her life, the church could not make it on its own anymore, so it had to merge with another congregation in a nearby town. Reluctantly, Grandma gave up her church home where everything significant in her whole life had happened, and moved her membership to the new church. But she was still with people she knew and loved, and even though it was a major loss for her, she adjusted well and got involved in her new church home. A few months after she died, an arsonist struck her old church in the middle of the night, and all that was left standing were a couple of stone walls. It made the loss even more final for many of us, as that building symbolized an important part of our home in the past. It gives me a taste of what the Israelites must have felt in exile—not only did they lose people they loved in Babylonia's military action against them, but they also were forced to abandon their homes and their Temple was destroyed.

In a word, that's grief for you. It is the loss of something you loved, something you needed and wanted but don't have anymore. The burning of that church symbolizes for me the destruction, helplessness, sorrow, anger, longing, questioning, and loss.

While sorting through Grandma's possessions, my mother found an old doll and gave it to my wife, who loves dolls. Now, when I say this doll was old, I'm being kind. My mother would not even touch it. It was triple wrapped in a garbage bag, like a mummy. When we opened it, we could see why. It looked like it had been a home for the mice for generations.

My wife worked hard to get her all cleaned up, and got her eyes looking out of the eye sockets again. She looked at old pictures of what those dolls looked like, and bought the right kind of wig and new clothing for her. She took her to a professional doll collector, who figured out that the doll is even older than Grandma was; it must have originally come from Germany in the early 1800s.

For me, the restoring of that doll, which seemed impossibly lost, is a symbol of what God can do for people in grief. When it feels like your whole world has fallen apart, when you have lost everything you consider home, then *God is able to make a new beginning out of any ending.* (The old church may have burned, but the congregation is still ministering in Christ's name.) And at the funeral, the minister looked out at all of her family and after talking about many of her good points, said, "You know, I can see a lot of her in all of you." Have faith in your joys, and even during your sorrows. God is able to make a new beginning out of any ending.

Let us pray:
Lord, be with those who are in grief in our community and world. Help us have the faith that you are still at work in our times of loss, bringing about new beginnings where we have only been able to see destruction and endings. Through Christ, our risen Savior. Amen.

READ IN YOUR BIBLE: *Psalm 119:33-40*

July 20, 2003

SUGGESTED PSALM: *Psalm 119:1-16*

SUGGESTED HYMNS:

   "Love Divine, All Loves Excelling" *(All)*
   "O Perfect Love" *(B, F, L, P, UM)*

Responding to God's Law

Hearing the Word

Psalm 119, the longest psalm in the Bible, is about the law of the Lord. It is carefully arranged as an acrostic poem, meaning that the first letter in each line begins with the letters of the alphabet, arranged in alphabetical order. This psalm is a variation on that because there are eight lines for each letter, resulting in the long length of the psalm. Of course, the poem uses the letters of the Hebrew alphabet, and so the acrostic nature of the poem is lost in translation to English. Using an acrostic form of poetry was probably a memory aid, but it could also express a sense of completeness; for every situation you could imagine, the law of the Lord is adequate. In Nehemiah 8 (the lesson scripture), the Law is read and interpreted to the people following their time in the exile, when they would not have been able to congregate and study it as they could in the promised land.

Living the Word

Driving to Quincy, Illinois, from Camp Point, my wife and I noticed what appeared to be a traffic jam ahead on Highway 24. As we got closer, we saw a small orange sign on the road telling us what was ahead. In the town of Coatsburg, the Illinois State Police had set up a roadside check. That meant if you were going to proceed west on Highway 24, you had to stop and talk to the state troopers. They would check your driver's license, make sure you were wearing a seat belt, make sure you were not intoxicated, check to see if you are wearing bank robber masks, and so forth.

Of course, all this takes time. The line was long, and we were in a hurry. There was a turnoff for a blacktop road that would get us to Quincy between us and the start of the long line, so I took that instead of waiting in line for the traffic check.

Later a friend said that he had been listening on his police scanner. The police apparently expected people to do exactly what we did, and particularly people who had some reason to dodge the police. At least one of their objectives was apparently to watch the people who turned away! They had a hidden policeman with binoculars running checks on the license plates of the cars that took the alternate route! I remember thinking at the time that they should have put the traffic checkpoint somewhere besides a place where you could see it and turn away from it. What criminal is going to voluntarily drive up to the police, roll down his or her window, hand the police their driver's license, and say, "Hi officers! If this car happens to show up as a stolen vehicle, believe me, I just bought it from a guy who told me it's a real steal. I thought it seemed suspicious at the time, and so I was just now looking for you guys to report it stolen, and what a coincidence, here you are!"

When I read the part of Psalm 119:33 that said, "Teach me, Lord, the meaning of your laws, and I will obey them at all times," at first it struck me as funny. After all, maybe car thieves just need someone to sit down with them and carefully explain to them that theft would apply in the case of driving off with someone else's Mercedes without their permission. No, the Illinois State Police know that obedience to the law is more than an educational problem! It is a problem of the will. We see the law, we know the law; but we continue to break the law, and we avoid the law. That's human nature. The problem is more than understanding the law; the problem is that we have the will to rebel against it.

When I read the Psalm again, though, I could see it was not attempting to describe the world as it is; it was attempting to describe the world the way it should be. We should want to keep the law, for the law is good. We should live in such a way that it would be fine with us to go through the traffic stop. God's law, like Illinois State law, is meant to promote good things. Why go around that which is there to help you live a better life?

Let us pray:
Lord, thank you for your law, which instructs us in the right way and convicts us when we stray from your path. Give us not only the knowledge of your ways, but also the will to follow them, for our good and your greater glory. Amen.

SUGGESTED HYMNS:
  "More Love to Thee, O Christ" (B, C, F, P, UM)
  "There's a Wideness in God's Mercy" (All)

Renewing Spiritual Commitments

Hearing the Word

Psalm 66:8-20 paints the picture of a person who has gone through a difficult time, during which he made a vow to God that if God would help him out of the situation, he would make special sacrifices for God. Known as "bargaining with God," this is a common part of human suffering. This man, however, was in the process of keeping his part of the bargain, for God had rescued him from his troubles. In today's lesson scripture from Nehemiah, the people of Israel have been through the exile, and now that they are back in the promised land they enter into a new promise with God, renewing their covenant relationship with God.

Living the Word

Two preachers are having coffee in a local restaurant, as is their usual weekly custom. On this day they get into an energetic discussion about the best posture for prayer. One points out, "The best way to pray is to kneel and close your eyes."

The other pastor replies, "That's fine for some people, but when you really want to get to the highest levels of being in the Spirit, you have to be on your feet so you can move around as the Spirit leads you. And you should put your hands up in the air, reaching out for God like a child reaches out for their loving parent."

"No," countered the other one, "in all the pictures you see of Jesus praying, he is on his knees with his eyes closed."

An electrician had been rewiring an outlet nearby, and listening in on their conversation. Finally he said, "Excuse me, guys, but you're both wrong. I've tried it both of the ways you are talking about, and I can tell you that the most fervent position for prayer is when your feet kick out when you're climbing an electric pole, and you are hanging upside down by a safety strap right over high voltage lines. That's definitely the best position for a heartfelt prayer that I know."

When there is time, it is common to bargain with God in such situations. An old joke has two men lost at sea, holding onto a piece of their wrecked boat, with sharks circling all around. One of them is praying aloud, "Oh God, if you get us out of this mess, I promise I'll go to church from now on, both services, and I'll teach Sunday school too! I promise I'll give up all my bad habits, and I'll quit swearing. I promise I'll give half of my money to the poor, and I promise not to complain about it either. I promise I'll quit watching ball games all weekend and instead I'll do all the fix-up things around the house my wife wants me to do. I promise."

Suddenly his friend interrupts him. "Hey, you'd better stop right there before you completely ruin your life. Here comes the Coast Guard."

Sometimes people keep the bargains they make with God in times of trouble, but usually the promises we make voluntarily, without feeling threatened, are the ones we are most likely to keep. The man who wrote the psalm seemed cheerful about making a costly sacrifice at the temple following his close call and bargain. It is good that he kept his word, and was cheerful about it. What is better is that he realized that God was faithful to him, and he felt grateful for it.

Our faith is really not a matter of striking a bargain with God, as though we had to negotiate against someone whose interests are opposite our own. The best promises are the ones God makes to us, and the second best are the commitments we make in response, not to terror, but to the love of God for us.

Let us pray:
Lord, thank you for your faithfulness to us; even your willingness to stand by and wait for us to turn to you, even if you must endure decades of being ignored. Guide us in making commitments that are helpful and meaningful. May our commitments to you not feel like a burden, but a joy and an opportunity to express our gratefulness to you. Amen.

SUGGESTED HYMNS:
  "There Is a Balm in Gilead" (B, E, F, P, UM, W)
  "Come, Thou Fount of Every Blessing" (B, C, E, F, L, P, UM)

Peril of Pride

Hearing the Word

Again, these words from Isaiah come from the portion of Isaiah written after the exile (chapters 40 and following). They are reassuring, pastoral words of hope and comfort for a suffering people. They affirm the special relationship that God has with Israel as opposed to other nations (Egypt and Ethiopia are specifically mentioned), and indicates that the purpose for this special relationship is for them to bring God glory (on this, see especially 43:7). They also promise that the people of Israel will be gathered from distant places and allowed to return to the promised land.

Living the Word

One day it rained hard here in Camp Point. For several hours, it came down like we have never seen it before, and in the ditches the water came up. It came up like we have never seen it before. At first, it was a novelty. After it slacked off, the kids pulled off their shoes and socks and went wading on our driveway. We took pictures, the neighbors came out and we walked around, marveling at how high the water had suddenly gotten.

Then the skies darkened again, we all ran for cover, and another huge deluge of rain swept through the area. Soon the water was nearly up to the floorboard of our car in the driveway. But the waters were not finished rising. It is amazing how fast water can rise when you are not ready for it, and it is amazing how many tools and unpacked boxes of clothes and trash bags and other things were sitting on the floor of our garage when the water reached the top of the driveway and began to run across the floor.

By now, we were working hard and fast because the water completely covered the garage floor. As it approached the metal threshold between the garage and entry into the house, I hurriedly grabbed a tube of caulking and laid a thick and sloppy layer of caulk all around that threshold and a board I propped up against it to gain a little bit of height. Real panic and disorganization began to set in as the water began to lap at the new caulking. It alone now protected the family room, my office, the downstairs storage and bedroom areas, all of which were right through that opening. They were carpeted, and were filled with lots of things such as file cabinets and chairs and wooden furniture that we did not want to have sitting in water. Then, about the time the panic had changed to helplessness, the rain stopped and the water quit rising.

This scripture compares rising flood waters with troubles, and it is a good analogy. Some troubles start small, but any problem can be the last straw, the water spilling over their last vain hope to avert tragedy. Troubles can overwhelm people, like flood waters can simply run under, over, or through a levy.

We build all kinds of levies in life to try to keep trouble away. We save money for a rainy day, we buy insurance for every peril our agent can make us afraid of, we put on a seatbelt, we lock the doors, we eat right, and so on. But sometimes, in spite of our best efforts, the levy breaks anyway. The floods come and level our castles of sand, the parts of our life we thought were protected. In these moments consolation comes, not from being told that it could have been worse, but from knowing that someone is there with you in the mess. When the floods of life come, when all the things that we thought protected us and made us invincible have failed us, when we are left with nothing, we still have the Lord, who loves us. That is the presence that can give us hope, for once the whole earth was covered in raging water, and just look what God has been able to make out of that mess! So do not be afraid. God is truly with you, and at his command, the waters will part and a new life will begin.

Let us pray:

Lord, when the people and things that we counted on for our happiness and security fail us, then we ask that you help us through. Thank you for being there for us, not to claim that the mess is not so bad, but to make sure we do not go through it alone. In Christ, who walked on the water and calmed the storm, we pray. Amen.

READ IN YOUR BIBLE: *Acts 2:14-23, 32-33*   **August 10, 2003**
SUGGESTED PSALM: *Psalm 68:1-10*
SUGGESTED HYMNS:
  "Blessed Assurance" (B, C, F, P, UM)
  "Breathe on Me, Breath of God" (B, E, F, L, P, UM, W)

Call to Repentance

Hearing the Word

After Jesus had risen from the dead and appeared to many people, and then ascended into heaven, the coming of the Holy Spirit on the gathered believers marked what we call Pentecost. It was a way that the Spirit of God returned to enliven the believers and give them a new sense of mission. This sudden manifestation of God's presence included speaking in foreign languages, which should be contrasted to the Tower of Babel story in Genesis 11. It evoked questions from onlookers, and so Peter interpreted the event in light of Joel's prophecy (which is the lesson scripture for the day).

Living the Word

When I turned the key in the ignition, I got no response at all. The lights would not come on either, so I knew the battery was probably dead. "Dead" is a good word to describe not only the battery, but also the whole vehicle when the battery is discharged. It is amazing how quiet and lifeless everything in the car is without the battery; no lights flicker on, no dashboard indicators are working, and of course, there is only quiet when you are used to hearing the engine fire up. Every element in the whole engine can be in fine working order, but without the battery, it will just sit there.

Anyway, it was time to break out the jumper cables! That may seem like a good task for a mechanic, but I think it is basically a theological act. After all, the jumper cables transfer life and energy and power from the car with the live battery to the car that is dead. And when you are done, you have gotten the dead car to fire up! What's more theological than that?

Pentecost is a lot like starting a car with a dead battery. The gathered disciples, before Pentecost, had all the equipment they needed to do God's work; they just needed to receive the power to do it. Even for us still today, God is like the live battery that we need to be connected in order to receive the power we need to come to life! Without that power in our life, we are like a perfectly good engine that cannot do the job it was made for.

Once the car is started, then what? We start a car in order for it to take us somewhere. We have a journey in mind, a reason to bring the engine to life. In the same way, God has given us his spirit in order to fulfill purposes, not just to feel all excited with no place to go! Some Christians, I think, approach worship that way. They want to experience an emotional high, a powerful connection to the Almighty God, and after singing and praising they have indeed felt God's power. They are all revved up. Then they shut off the engine and head out the door of the church!

However, God wanted to start up the engine so that we might be able to get going out there in the world! God has given us power through his life-giving Spirit so we would have the energy and the vitality we need to strengthen the lonely and weak, resist temptation, comfort the grieving, feed and clothe the poor, and make new disciples for Christ. If we never do these things, or do God's work in some way, then we are like a car that is on sale in a mall. Every once in a while the engine is started up just so people can hear the engine, but the car itself does not move an inch. The engine roars to life, but doesn't do anything except make noise!

Pentecost should remind us that God is all powerful, and we are dead without God. It should also remind us that God didn't bring us to life just to make a bunch of noise; he has a journey he wants to take, and he needs us to be like a car that will start, and once started, will go places.

Let us pray:
Lord, we confess that sometimes we feel spiritually dead, like a car engine that will not even make a sound, we have lost the power to do anything when we have lost our connection with you. Strengthen that bond between you and us, Lord, that we might be enlivened by your presence in our life, and guided by your hand as we give all of our power to doing your will. Amen.

READ IN YOUR BIBLE: *Psalm 90:1-17*　　　　**August 17, 2003**
SUGGESTED PSALM: *Psalm 139*
SUGGESTED HYMNS:
  "O God, Our Help in Ages Past" (All)
  "God of Grace and God of Glory" (B, C, E, F, L, P, UM)

Different Destinies

Hearing the Word

Psalm 90 is a beautiful poetic expression, full of wisdom. While Christians are used to thinking of life after death as heaven, some strands of Jewish thought (not all) understood human life as strictly temporary, with no afterlife. The only way to live on after death was through male descendants because they would carry on the family name, and thus the enduring memory of that family would keep them alive in other people's minds. This understanding of the (absence of an) afterlife helps explain why it was so important for couples to have male children in that society, and why the inability of a woman to bear a male child was thought to be a sign that God was displeased (thus denying them ongoing life). It also placed a high value on appreciating this present life, which is evident in this Psalm. Note the absence of any mention of heaven; instead, God alone is eternal, and humans are mortal.

Living the Word

One day my wife asked me to come outside to see what she had been doing in the backyard. She had been painting a wood wagon under the shade of the big old locust tree. None of that struck me as remarkable or even interesting enough for her to have me come out to look. Then she pointed out the big tree limb lying in pieces on the ground. It had fallen out of the tree and landed right next to her. She said that she heard the crack above her, but didn't know which way to move. So she stayed put. If she had moved one step to the right, it would be a different story.

It is likely that the older we become, the more close-call stories we could tell. Sometimes we aren't aware of close calls, sometimes we are.

105

Even the constancy of the environment upon which all of life depends relies almost entirely on the danger inherent in close calls not coming to pass. For example, solar storms fairly regularly emit bursts of radiation powerful enough to temporarily shut down or damage satellites in space. If a human being happened to be up on that satellite during such a storm, it would give them radiation poisoning, or maybe even kill them instantly. The only thing protecting us on earth from these outbursts is our atmosphere, but a really powerful solar storm could change all that, and make earth more like—well—Mars. No extinction-causing meteors or comets have struck the earth in many millions of years, but if they ever do, it won't matter if you're insured against it! All of them are highly unlikely, but they do serve to remind us that life is here, fragile as it is, because we as a planet have successfully navigated a minefield of earth-altering catastrophes in the past few million years.

Tidal waves, volcanic blasts, hurricanes, tornadoes are all just hiccups on the surface of the earth, but many lives depend on these things not happening on any given day.

Living would be needlessly stressful if we dwelled on all the perils of life. But this psalm reminds us that any individual human being has at best a life that seems quite short. This sense of mortality could frighten us, but our Christian understanding of heaven is comforting and gives this short life an entirely different perspective. Yet even without our Christian belief in heaven, the writer of Psalm 90 still has a healthy and wise attitude about the brevity of life. He encourages us to enjoy it, appreciate it, and remember that even though we are temporary, God is everlasting. Even knowing that heaven is waiting for us someday, it is still a foolish waste to spend any day pouting or angry or complaining. Instead, let us be wise enough to thank God in the morning for the opportunity another day of life brings, and make the best use of it we can. It is far better to use a gift well than to insult the giver by throwing it away.

Let us pray:
Lord, help me appreciate this day that you have given me. Keep me from choosing any attitude that would tarnish its beauty. Instead, may my life be used by you to make this day a special one for others as I seek to love and to serve, just as Jesus taught us to spend our precious days. Amen.

READ IN YOUR BIBLE: *Revelation 21:1-7*   **August 24, 2003**

SUGGESTED PSALM: *Psalm 140*

SUGGESTED HYMNS:

   "This Is My Father's World" (B, C, E, F, L, P, UM)

   "Hope of the World" (E, L, P, UM, W)

Certainty in
an Uncertain World

Hearing the Word

Revelation is the last book in the New Testament, not because it was the latest one written, but because it deals with John's vision of the last things (the end of this world and the beginning of a new one). In it, God is portrayed as overwhelmingly powerful in order to encourage Christians who are undergoing persecution and paints a picture of the power of God. God's power dwarfs the so-called power of the civil leaders who are intimidating Christians by the threat of persecution. It is a way of saying, "God will get them in the end, and so if you stick with the right side, you will eventually be vindicated." Daniel is another book of the Bible that speaks to those who are being persecuted for their faith (even though it is located in the Old Testament).

Living the Word

I read with concern one report after another by various scientific and environmental groups regarding the dwindling status of many of the earth's animals, plants, and other natural resources. The World Conservation Union's Species Survival Commission publishes one such report, known as the "Red List," every few years. This massive study is comprised of about seven thousand scientific experts from all over the world. As of 2000, there are more than eleven thousand different kinds of plants and animals that we may permanently say farewell to in the next few years.

Behind many of these threatened species there are more complex economic, political, and international questions, but most of them boil down to a struggle that pits what is good financially for some people against what is good for the environment.

Suppose the scientists turn out to be right, or even half right, and lots of plants and animals become extinct in the coming decades. Is there any hope? It depends on what you hope for. To hope this will have no impact on humans is folly. The real question is what the impact will be. The loss of some kinds of whales will hurt the whaling industry (it already has). The loss of certain kinds of sharks may only affect people who like shark fin soup. On the other hand, we don't really know what would happen if you remove sharks from their role at the top of the ocean's food chain. The loss of sharks might indeed have devastating effects on all forms of ocean life.

I'm optimistic enough to hope that after we have lost enough treasured species (gorillas, tigers, rhinos, and others we know from zoos), maybe humans will develop enough political will to protect the rest of them and the rate of loss will stabilize. Others are not so optimistic; they predict the issues of overpopulation and environmental misuse will eventually threaten humans too, or that we may reach a point at which the biodiversity upon which the current world ecosystem depends will collapse, taking a terrible toll on the human population in the form of disease and starvation. I hope such dire predictions never come to pass, but to me, even the loss of the chance for our grandchildren to see rainforests, or to benefit from the cure to some type of cancer that may be found in the plants that we are now losing, is a price too high.

In Revelation, our Creator says, "I am the first and the last, the beginning and the end." The Lord was pleased to create each one of these eleven thousand endangered plants and animals. He looked at them, and said, "It is good." And God will still be hovering nearby as the last one takes its final breath.

Let's have faith, and let's also work to stop the destruction. It's just showing a little respect for God's awesome works of art.

Let us pray:
Lord, help us appreciate your brilliance and creativity expressed in each plant and animal around us. May we find hope in your endless creativity, knowing that even in the midst of death and destruction, you are able to make all things new. Amen.

Final Rewards

Hearing the Word

The heavenly scene of the throne of God and the attending court is one that is used in other places in the Bible (compare it, for example, to Isaiah 6). It is important to keep in mind the intended reader, who is afraid of the persecution of Christians. The effect of such a scene would be to give a reassuring mental image to the person who is afraid. When this book is used to frighten people with its powerful scenes, it is using it to convey a message that is exactly the opposite of the comforting, encouraging, and motivating message it was intended to have. Note verse 14, which mentions that the people in good standing in heaven have "safely come through the terrible persecution." Remember that these words may be read by people who have lost a family member or friend to persecution, and it makes them wonder, Will I be next? and Is my faith really worth dying for?

Living the Word

Overheard being said by a restless child in church during the sermon: "Mom and Dad, if we give him the money now, will he quit talking and let us go home?"

Like this child did, adults wonder when the end of the story will come, too, and what it will be like. Some people think the book of Revelation is a roadmap in code, telling us everything that will happen (it is filled with symbols and strange images that invite a variety of meanings). Some people, as they consider Revelation, seem to think that all we have to do is break the code, and then we will have been given advance knowledge of the events that will lead to the end of the world.

Sometimes I hear a minister on television who actually seems to relish interpreting today's world events and making them fit various parts of Revelation. Then using other parts he predicts what will happen; his basic point always seems to be that "This proves the end of the world is near." From his perspective, that is a good thing, because it means that the return of Christ is close at hand.

While I agree that the return of Christ will be a good thing (at least for those with whom Christ is pleased) I do not agree with that method of understanding the book of Revelation. First, it cheapens the message of the book and reduces it to a book that is supposed to give us a godlike understanding of future events. Instead, it was written to help the original readers who were undergoing persecution have courage in a hostile world to help them cling to their faith when their lives were threatened, when their loved ones were being taken from them, and when they were going through a time of severe testing. This book was meant to say, "Our God is stronger than any force in the world today. Therefore you can trust God. The real end is not death, but life beyond death when our powerful God will vindicate the faithful and punish the evil ones. Therefore, stay firm in your faith even to death if need be, because it is faithfulness, and not just avoiding death, that gives the real victory in the end."

In America, we are not threatened with death for gathering to worship or for possessing a Bible. But there are definitely times in our life when we need to have courage against evil forces. There are times when life seems to fall apart and have no hope. We need to remember that God is stronger than any of the difficult circumstances of this world. God is able to give a victory in the end to all the faithful, and to defeat evil in all of its various forms.

Revelation tells us that God is still in charge, and determined to bring about justice, peace, a world without grief or pain, and genuine love in all its fullness. In short, God wants to bring about the kingdom of God. In that kingdom, every problem we face now will be left behind. A truly happy day is coming, and that day will last forever.

Let us pray:
Lord, help us trust you with a future we cannot see, and know that all the difficulties we face in this world will fade away in the radiant glory of your coming kingdom of eternal joy, love, and peace. May we remain faithful to you in all things, this day as then. Amen.